"I applaud Steve's courage and profes[...] much needed book. The church is mad[...] illness is a real problem that cannot be swept under the rug. As God gave us doctors to help us with heart attacks, back surgeries, and diabetes, he also gave us doctors to help us with mental illness. Of course God can heal somebody immediately of any disease or illness, but oftentimes he uses doctors, medicine, and other tools to help. In that regard, I believe Steve's book is a godsend. It gives pastors the knowledge, information, and tools they need to successfully and confidently address this critical issue with those they oversee. God bless you Steve for having the courage to come out of the darkness and shine a light on your own experience so that others may be helped, healed, blessed, and God glorified throughout. Steve Bloem delivers the information in a way that will help pastors and impact the kingdom of God today and in the ages to come. God has used Steve's personal journey mightily to help him understand the tragedy, effects, trauma, solutions, and answers for dealing with mental illness. This book is a must read for every pastor, and I believe should be taught as a course in every seminary."

—Jack Alan Levine,
Executive Pastor, Purpose Church,
Orlando, Florida

"I have been a pastor and a seminary professor for many years, and I don't think I've ever encountered a book as helpful, as complete, and as biblical as Steve Bloem's *The Pastoral Handbook of Mental Illness: A Guide for Training and Reference.* This will become one of the most important books in your library. Steve Bloem is incredibly knowledgeable and refreshingly authentic. The compassion and sensitivity of these pages is Christlike. Get this book and, when you do, you'll thank me for having commended it to you."

—Steve Brown,
Professor of Practical Theology Emeritus,
Reformed Theological Seminary

"In Steve Bloem's latest book, T*he Pastoral Handbook of Mental Illness*, he draws from pastoral training and experience, plus years of professional mental health training and counseling experience to synthesize practical knowledge about mental health issues within the church that local pastors face today. Steve also gives the reader insight into his own personal struggle with mental illness and how it affected him and his family. Mental illness affects not only the individual with the diagnosis but the person's family as well. This book will help church leaders to better understand mental illness and how the church family can lovingly extend compassion and understanding to those who are affected by this disease."

—Gene Pearson,
Pastor of Care and Counseling,
Rush Creek Bible Church,
Byron Center, Michigan

"Every pastor needs to own this book. Here's why. Thankfully, in recent years, our western church culture has taken some steps forward in understanding mental illness but we have a long way to go. Steve Bloem helps us move further faster by challenging us with insights from Scripture many of us have simply ignored. Yes, that's right, the Bible talks about mental illness and the scope is significant. In addition, this is a handbook. It is a quick reference that provides us with both an introductory understanding of various mental illnesses, along with guides for helping us respond to those struggling. This is a book written from both an academic and a life-lived perspective. Steve and his wife Robyn weave their own personal stories throughout its pages, helping us gain a greater understanding and providing us with the necessary resources to make wise responses to those afflicted with mental illness."

—Ken Taylor,
Founding and Teaching Pastor,
Creekside Church, Waterloo, Ontario

The

PASTORAL
HANDBOOK
of
MENTAL
ILLNESS

A Guide for Training and Reference

STEVE BLOEM

The Pastoral Handbook of Mental Illness: A Guide for Training and Reference
© 2018 by Steve Bloem

Published by Kregel Publications, a division of Kregel Inc., 2450 Oak Industrial Dr. NE, Grand Rapids, MI 49505–6020.

Scripture quotations are from the New American Standard Bible®. Copyright © 1960, 1962, 1963, 1968, 1971, 1972, 1973, 1975, 1977 by The Lockman Foundation. Used by permission. www.Lockman.org.

Scripture quotations marked KJV are from the King James Version.

The Hebrew font, NewJerusalemU, and the Greek font, GraecaU, are available from www.linguistsoftware.com/lgku.htm, +1-425-775-1130.

ISBN 978–0–8254–4466–1

Printed in the United States of America

18 19 20 21 22 / 5 4 3 2 1

I dedicate this book to Robyn,
who is my soulmate,
my confidant,
the love of my life,
the wonderful Mother of our children,
and a helper in all my endeavors.

CONTENTS

WHY WRITE A HANDBOOK FOR PASTORS ABOUT MENTAL ILLNESS?

Dr. D. Martyn Lloyd-Jones was a medical doctor and a very effective pastor/ teacher. He knew the importance of having a book in print that would aid pastors to clearly differentiate between spiritual and medical issues, and avoided the one-size-fits-all mentality. I submit a paragraph from his writing:

> Having insured that the approach has been right, we come to the actual diagnosis. If you cannot make a diagnosis you cannot help your patient. Here again lies the importance of an accurate knowledge of the facts, the facts of life and the spiritual facts. They all come together here. To me the thing that is needed above everything else at the present time is an accurate textbook which deals with the borderland where the spiritual, the psychological, and the psychiatric meet. This is the most difficult sphere of all in the practice of medicine, and in Christian pastoral work. I have thought about it for some forty-five years, for ministers have been in the habit of sending people to me and explaining, "I don't know what to think of this case, is it a spiritual or a psychological one?" There is really no adequate textbook on this problem, and it is very important from every standpoint. Much time will be lost if you cannot differentiate. You will be unhelpful to the person who is confronting you and perhaps even harmful.[1]

This book is being written so that pastors, deacons, and other Christian workers might know how to help people who have mental illness. It is meant to be in all cultures, since mental illness knows no boundaries. I believe that a correct biblical theology includes validating mental illness as a true disease entity as well as securing the appropriate help for those who are suffering from it. In this book, we will discuss how to identify the signs and symptoms of mental illness, using the historical principle of "check the first symptoms." Early intervention is important because depression, bipolar disease, and other disorders are neurodegenerative diseases; getting speedy treatment not only relieves the intensity and severity of one's suffering, but many times saves lives. It is a fact that one of the first stops for a suicidal, depressed person is the pastor's office. Many pastors, because of their lack of familiarity with mental illness, miss the real problem and offer some encouragement from Scripture such as "David encouraged himself in the LORD his God" (1 Sam. 30:6, KJV); "Be anxious for nothing" (Philippians 4:6); or "I will fear no evil . . . thy rod and thy staff they comfort me" (Psalm 23, KJV). I have used all of the above in my fight against depression; but we must remember that Romans 8:10 also tells us, "the body is dead because of sin, but the Spirit is life because of righteousness." These diseases called mental illnesses result from malfunctioning of the brain, which in turn affects the intellect, the emotions, and the will.

Mental illness is a full-body disease. It affects the vegetative functioning of the sufferer, who either eats nothing or too much, and cannot sleep or sleeps too much; his sex drive is either very weak or very strong; his internal clock (circadian rhythm) is not functioning properly; he cannot concentrate. There are others who may be hearing voices (which are not from the devil), and others who are sure they are having a heart attack; they become somatically preoccupied. Some have developed defense mechanisms; a common one is "a smiling depression." Another problem people have is that they lack insight into the real problem. This is called *anosognosia*. We may feel someone is "just in denial," but *anosognosia* is a medical term from the Greek that means "to not know a disease." When a person has a mental illness, they cannot always perceive their condition accurately. This is more common in some mental disorders than in others. Sometimes a person's awareness can switch back and forth, making us think they are just being stubborn, when this *anosognosia* is actually evidence of the disease.

This manual will help you identify mental illnesses and their symptoms, to understand what to do when a person is suicidal, to biblically encourage and comfort the sufferer, and to make the choice of whether you can handle the problem yourself or if you need to refer the person to appropriate mental health professionals.

This manual will also help you to have a biblical, pastoral theology—one that does not get caught up in "one size fits all." It will also unravel the differences (and similarities) between spiritual depression and bereavement or grief reactions. In my private practice, I have helped many people identify their mental illnesses. I have been able to get them treatment quickly, while continuing to give them biblical counseling as well as a clinical understanding of their mental illness. Job, no doubt, had a trifold depression and was deeply affected by great losses. One of the severest attacks launched against him was by his friends, who considered themselves his counselors. He stands as a testimony through the ages of a person who endured astounding satanic attacks; because of his unswerving fidelity to God and His purposes, his book has been a help to many who suffer.

In my research, I have been unable to find a satisfactory definition of what I consider to be pastoral theology. This is my own definition: Pastoral theology is the systemization of the truth of Scripture regarding the pastoral care of the believer. This would include the application of biblical principles and truths to the needs of the flock, answering their soul's questions, helping them cope in trials and temptations, and otherwise shepherding the flock of God for the generation in which we live.

I spend many hours each week meeting with people who have all sorts of mental illnesses, and am able to comfort them with the comfort that I have received in the Lord. My wife, Robyn, does the same. Another of my burdens, and therefore a task I deal with regularly, is to refute teachers who are in error regarding the causes and cures of mental illness. I do this with biblical principles and facts about these diseases. People who have a mental health diagnosis need an informed godly advocate who will help them when the environment becomes too powerful for them to overcome.

What is a pastoral theology? It is a theology based on the exposition of the Bible and the careful application of truth for the generation in which we live. The Ephesian pastors were called by the apostle Paul to Miletus:

> And when they had come to him, he said to them, "You yourselves know, from the first day that I set foot in Asia, how I was with you the whole time, serving the Lord with all humility and with tears and with trials which came upon me through the plots of the Jews; how I did not shrink from declaring to you anything that was profitable, and teaching you publicly and from house to house" (Acts 20:18–20).

In the New American Standard Bible, Paul uses the term "how I did not shrink."[2] He never tried to hedge on the Word of God, knowing that all Scripture is profitable. He was a bondservant of Christ and his concern was to deliver the Word of God. This is true of any doctrine that is taught in the Bible. The tendency is to come out from under the Word of God and pull back from some particular teaching because it might be too controversial. We should not love a fight, but consider our duty to fight against error.

If one finds himself omitting important doctrines from one's preaching, he had better examine himself. The Word of God is "God-breathed" in every part and word. This is called the verbal, plenary inspiration of the Bible. We must preach what He has declared!

The reason Robyn and I founded Heartfelt Counseling Ministries, and its extension ministry CAMI (Christians Afflicted with Mental Illness), was to educate and advocate for the mentally ill. We chose the name CAMI after much prayer and thought. We use the word "afflicted" because we believe so strongly that mental illness is an affliction to be treated, and not a failure of character or ambition. This is also why we have started CAMI support groups, with written material and leaders trained to help others. They use our CAMI leader guides and student guides, with weekly lessons, to learn how to support each other through the episodic downturns of depression and other mental illnesses. There is no cure—it can only be managed—and everyone needs helpful and educated supporters.

There are many erroneous teachings surrounding mental illness, which cause people to spend massive amounts of money to believe things that simply are not true! The result is that the people who are sick do not improve, and are not able to serve in their local church or fulfill their familial tasks. In my own experience, I have seen people who were treated so harshly by the church body and its leadership that they just stopped going to church all together. The pastor must be able to address those in the church who wish to thwart ministry to those who have mental illness. He also needs to exhort and comfort both the caregiver in the congregation and the mentally ill themselves.

Paul's instruction to Titus helps us understand what to do with the two groups above. Paul tells Titus, in 1:9, "Holding fast (αφντεχοτωμενον[3]) the faithful word[4] which is in accordance with the teaching, so that he will be able both to exhort, (παρακαλειν[5]) in sound doctrine and to refute εφλετωγχειν[6] those who contradict αφντιλετωγοντα.[7] What are needed are a concept of edification and the fighting of error. Another way of explaining this uses the analogy of the sword and the trowel. Some pastors spend all their time building up their people (the trowel); other pastors spend all their time refuting or convicting of error (the sword). Both must be used in an effective ministry. Ephesians 4:15 states, "But speaking the truth in love, we are to grow up in all aspects into Him who is the head, even Christ."

Pastoral theology is a discipline which studies the Bible and the human heart. When I was junior in college I had the opportunity to speak with J. I. Packer, and asked him for some pastoral advice. He told me, "Know two books: the Bible and the human heart." He went on to say, "Don't be a cardboard man; be a three-dimensional man." Pastors have to leave the study and interact with God's people.

Mentally ill people need empathy and compassion. The most effective pastors in this case would be known as wounded healers. I hope to see more people with depression and other mental illnesses step out to start churches and to pastor existing churches. In a future chapter, I will discuss having the office of a counseling pastor as a position in the local church. The problem with these important goals is that many pastors, including myself, have been overlooked in regard to pastoral positions because they have a disease—a disease that they would never have chosen, and one that is so often misunderstood. The stigma surrounding mental illness is so great that as soon as a person shows signs of depression, et cetera, on the mission field, the agency will almost always order him and his family home, with no real possibility of returning.

The apostle Paul was not ashamed of his depression or the depression of his fellow missionaries. He starts one of his most personal letters with the horror of what they experienced in Asia. Paul had a story of grace to tell. This passage revolutionizes teaching about believers in Christ who are suffering:

> For we do not want you to be unaware, brethren, of our affliction which came to us in Asia, so that we despaired even of life (2 Cor. 1:8).

Paul wanted the brothers and sisters in Christ to know not only his level of stress and suffering but also the terror of it. He knew it would help others going through life's sufferings and pain, and it would also cause them to pray for him and his fellow missionaries. Please see 2 Corinthians 1:11. His was a suffering that he describes as being far beyond human strength to endure.[8] Paul uses words that underscore the extent of his suffering. He uses hyperbole. He also says that "we were burdened excessively, *beyond our strength*." These last three words demonstrate that this was an unusual trial that was far beyond their ability to endure it. He also said that he "despaired even of life."

It was a suffering that the apostle said was like a death sentence. Second Corinthians 1:9 states, "indeed we had the sentence of death within ourselves." The Greek word for "had" carries the idea of still having a vivid recollection of that experience.[9] In today's language, we could say that the missionaries had PTSD.

The great lesson here, for our purposes, is that when a person is biologically or spiritually depressed to this point, they can look to God and know that not only the type of suffering but also the deliverance that will come is from a merciful and loving Father. God is a great deliverer of His suffering people. Paul goes on to talk about God's deliverance from sorrow, grief and depression, by he "who delivered us from so great a peril of death, and will deliver us, He on whom we have set our hope, and He will yet deliver us" (2 Cor. 1:10–11). It all became part of the Holy Writ. It has been tested throughout history that the compassionate, merciful Father has a way of delivering his people. Paul said that he had learned that the Lord had delivered them in the past, was delivering them in the present, and would deliver them in the future.[10]

The following quote from Lange's commentary is helpful on this passage.

> Of all persons in the world, the minister of Christ should know what true consolation and a cheerful spirit is. Only those who have comfort can impart it. A *theologus non tetanus*, a minister without an experience of personal trials in religion, lacks an important qualification for his work. The more afflictions, the more power he has; and the moment he enters the furnace of affliction, he has a virtual announcement from the Lord that some great work is before him, and that God is preparing him for higher usefulness. The soldier who is allowed to remain continually around the camp-fire will never learn true bravery. A minister's afflictions deepen the impression of his discourses. The admonitions of a veteran general have a power which no young captain can ever have.[11]

The Puritans show us what pastoral theology is all about. They knew the human heart and their preaching and writings demonstrate how well they were acquainted with the Bible. It has been estimated that the Puritans were not published after the mid 1800s. They pastored in the late 1500s until the early 1700s.[12] These pastors were experts of the soul and the Scriptures. We now have their works available to us. I particularly like *The Mute Christian and the Rod* by Thomas Brooks; *The Bruised Reed, the Soul's Conflict*, by Richard Sibbes and *The Reformed Pastor* by Richard Baxter. Thomas Manton and Thomas Goodwin also wrote a number of books on pastoral theology during this period of English History. A resurgence of the printing of the Puritans occurred in Great Britain in the late 1950s as a result of Dr. David Martyn Lloyd-Jones and others, who developed a Puritan Conference.[13]

SHEPHERD, AS LEADER

It is a pastoral theology that employs the metaphor of a shepherd for the leaders of Israel in the Old Testament, as well as for the pastor-teacher of the New Testament. One reason the Lord uses this metaphor is because sheep in many ways are fearful and helpless. Another reason the Lord uses this metaphor is because it demonstrates how the Lord, as our Shepherd, is full of tenderness and compassion toward his sheep. Another reason why the Lord uses the sheep metaphor is that he can use it as a model to teach and to chastise the leaders of Israel.

The shepherd/rulers in the Old Testament were often rebuked by the prophets for failing to humbly shepherd God's people. There is no hint in the Old Testament of a rancher driving his cattle. The need is for pastor/shepherds. The same is true in the New Testament. All through biblical history we see God using the shepherd metaphor to describe the role of men who would lead and teach the Word of God.

Another reason the Lord uses this metaphor is because sheep in many ways are fearful and helpless. Sheep tend to get themselves in trouble fast. In fact, when I was a missionary in Scotland as part of a Missionary Apprentice Team (MAP), I was eager to get a picture of a shepherd who was leading sheep home after grazing. I was so excited to get that perfect shot that I ran up to them with my camera. I immediately realized I had made a huge mistake; I startled the sheep. They began to run wildly everywhere; some even jumped over the wall and ran onto the nearby highway. The shepherd was visibly upset, with good cause, I might add. I felt terrible and apologized as he called them back and regathered his precious sheep. They sure are nervous creatures. But so are we.

Another reason why the Lord God of Israel used the sheep metaphor is because he will call his precious and true leaders shepherds, not the least being Jesus Christ who is also called the Good Shepherd (John 10) and the Great Shepherd of the sheep (Hebrews 13:20). We need the Good Shepherd, Jesus Christ, as Savior and Lord to lead and protect us.

Moses is a great example of a shepherd/leader. But he needed a lot of training by God for his leadership of Israel. Moses' life can be divided into three periods. His first forty years were in Pharaoh's household. Stephen, the "first martyr of the church," tells us:

> Moses was educated in all the learning of the Egyptians, and he was a man of power in words and deeds (Acts 7:22).

It is probable that Moses had been trained as an orator ("power in words") and he would also be trained as a military leader ("man of power) by men of war (Acts 7:20–29). God had a purpose for Moses getting this training. The original call came when he turned forty years old. At that point, he decided to become the deliverer of Israel. Hebrews tells us about his heart for the LORD God of Israel:

> By faith Moses, when he had grown up, refused to be called the son of Pharaoh's daughter, choosing rather to endure ill-treatment with the people of God than to enjoy the passing pleasures of sin, considering the reproach of Christ greater riches than the treasures of Egypt; for he was looking to the reward (Heb. 11:24–26).

Moses had seen the hard labor of his brethren, and witnessed an Egyptian beating a Hebrew. He looked around and when he thought no one was watching, he killed the Egyptian. The next day two Hebrews were fighting; Moses tried to intervene, when one of them said, "Who made you a prince or a judge over us? Are you intending to kill me as you did the Egyptian?" (Exod. 2:14a). Moses realized someone had seen him; and when Pharaoh heard about it, he tried to kill Moses. That is when Moses fled to Midian. Moses was trained for leadership by being a shepherd in obscurity.

Moses needed the training of a shepherd in the wilderness. After Moses fled Egypt he providentially came upon a shepherdess, Zipporah, when he defended her in a dispute over water. Her father, Jethro, heard about Moses' intervention and invited him for dinner. Eventually Moses married Zipporah, and for forty years worked for his father-in-law as a shepherd. At this time, being a shepherd was also a purposeful time of training. Strong military men do not make good shepherds unless they learn humility and nurturing from the Lord. Shepherding is hard, tedious work. Coming from the palace of Egypt it must have been especially abhorrent, since shepherds were despised in Egypt. During those long and laborious hours, days, and nights of shepherding, he must have thought many times, "What in the world am I doing here?" That is exactly what God wanted him to think; and it was the reason he was prepared for the next phase of his life. God uses weak men to accomplish his work. God came to him in the burning bush, and reminded him of his calling to deliver the people of Israel from Egypt.

Forty years is a long time, and Moses had probably given up what he thought was God's calling. Moses made many excuses as to why he should not be Israel's deliverer. These refusals angered the Lord, but finally Moses capitulated. God never wastes suffering, you can be sure of it. His providence not only brought Moses into the wilderness, so that he could learn through obscurity and loneliness, but when the time came, the LORD also brought him out of it. He would begin to understand, that he as a shepherd would know now that He would lead the people of Israel out of Egypt to the Promised Land, Canaan." The Scripture says:

> You led Your people like a flock by the hand of Moses and Aaron (Ps. 77:20).

The Exodus of Israel was in 1446 BC. As they left Egypt, their only visible connection with God was the pillar of cloud and pillar of fire. It was during this time that Moses received the law and the pattern for the Tabernacle. They spent about a year at the foot of Sinai. The LORD said to Moses:

> Let them construct a sanctuary for Me, that I may dwell among them. According to all that I am going to show you, as the pattern of the tabernacle and the pattern of all its furniture, just so you shall construct it (Exod. 25:8–9).

So now Moses the shepherd had to wander with the people for forty years in the wilderness. All the spies were killed except Joshua and Caleb. You probably don't remember the names of the ten spies because according to Proverbs 10:7, "The memory of the righteous is blessed, but the name of the wicked will rot."

Shepherding the mentally ill can be troublesome and exhausting, depending upon the severity of the illness. Many homeless people are mentally ill. What is our responsibility toward this population? Do we even have a responsibility? Who are the "least of these" whom Jesus spoke about? We have seen individuals who have families who live less than ten miles away.

Maybe their families have been burned out, and over time lost track of their cousin, brother, or even mother. These lost relatives are sometimes violent, and we understand that. That is why pastors and leaders need training.

At Heartfelt Counseling Ministries, we have a number of programs in place to reach out and stabilize the mentally ill. This type of advocacy should be familiar to those who are acquainted with the Old Testament. The Hebrew word *anah* and other related words tell us about God's view of helping those who are oppressed, bruised and poor in spirit. The mentally ill are certainly part of this populace. The study of this word and related words in the Old Testament is a wonderful way to prepare your heart and the hearts of your people to minister to the mentally ill.[14]

There are individuals who sit in your church every week, teach your Bible study classes, and sing in the choir. There are days they miss because of illness. The true reason they are not available is that they are in a depressive episode or experiencing a panic attack and they cannot get out of bed. The stigma and the judgmental attitudes they have encountered over the months and years of sickness have caused them to go into deep hiding. There are also people who have stopped going to church completely because they feel no one understands and they don't have the energy or resources to educate everyone. This is a major problem in our churches right now!

Moses' greatest test came after he had taken the people out of Egypt, and everything was ready for Israel to conquer Canaan. It was at Kadesh-Barnea that Moses sent twelve spies, one from each of the tribes of Israel, who carried on a reconnaissance maneuver in Canaan. When they returned with the report, ten of the twelve said it was filled with giants and that Israel would be defeated before them. The two who voted yes to go in were Caleb and Joshua. You probably don't remember the ten spies. God killed all ten of them and sentenced everyone in Israel twenty years and older to wander in the wilderness for forty years, until all had died.As they were poised for a second time to enter the land, the people began to carp and complain.

> So Moses took the rod from before the Lord, just as He had commanded him; and Moses and Aaron gathered the assembly before the rock. And he said to them, "Listen now, you rebels; shall we bring forth water for you out of this rock?" Then Moses lifted up his hand and struck the rock twice with his rod; and water came forth abundantly, and the congregation and their beasts drank. But the Lord said to Moses and Aaron, "Because you have not believed Me, to treat Me as holy in the sight of the sons of Israel, therefore you shall not bring this assembly into the land which I have given them" (Num. 20:9–12).

Moses had been a wonderful leader/shepherd to Israel, but on this occasion he had been hasty and passionate. He had been directed to *speak* to the rock but he *smote it twice* (Num. 20:11). His great mistake, as well as that of his brother Aaron, was that they represented the God of Israel as being harsh, rash, and full of anger when it came to blessing the people. The LORD showed his displeasure about sin in a leader. Moses knew he could not go into the Promised Land, but God took him to Mount Nebo and let him see the whole land of Canaan. Remember, leaders and teachers will be examined by the Lord as to how and what they taught the people. If you want to look at a sinless Prince and Shepherd there is only one, the theanthropic person, Jesus Christ. James 3:1 states, "Let not many of you become teachers, my brethren, knowing that as such we will incur a stricter judgment."

Moses asks the LORD to appoint a man over the congregation who should go out and in before them, and should lead them out and in, i.e., preside over and direct them in all their affairs. The words ובא and צאת ("go out," and "go in") are descriptions of the conduct of men in everyday life (Deut. 28:6; 31:2; Josh. 14:11). The words והביא and הוציא ("lead out and "bring in") signifies the superintendence of the affairs of the nation, and is founded upon the figure of a shepherd. One of the best descriptions of this "going out and in" that I found was in the Pulpit Commentary on Numbers 27:15:

> Which may go out before them, and which may go in before them. A comparison with the words of Moses in Deuteronomy 31:2, and of Caleb in Joshua 14:11, shows that the going out and coming in refer to the vigorous prosecution of daily business, and the fatigues of active service. Which may lead them out, and which may bring them in. The underlying image is that of a shepherd and his flock, which suggests itself so naturally to all that have the care and governance of men (cf. John 10:3, 4, 16). A people or nation who does not have a shepherd is therefore, helpless, bewildered, scattered, lost, and devoured. The image is frequent in Scripture (cf. 1 Kings 22:17; Ezekiel 34:5; Zechariah 10:2; Matthew 9:36).[15]

As pastors and as believers in Christ, we should seek to find our purpose in our own generation. I have had a number of pastorates. But over time, God led Robyn and me in a different direction. When we began to help people with mental illness, especially Christians, we saw His leading and blessing in ministry. We founded a nonprofit faith-based corporation called Heartfelt Counseling Ministries. It would not have been our first choice, but when God put a love in our heart toward people who are hurting, we knew someone needed what we had.

The Shepherd

The books of the Bible—including those that are historical, the wisdom literature books, the prophets, and the New Testament—all contain the shepherd model for leaders and pastors. There are many references in the Prophets about the shepherds/leaders of Israel. The prophet Ezekiel strongly rebuked the kings, who were often called shepherds. He charged them with not feeding the sheep but feeding themselves. He rebuked the "so-called shepherds" for not strengthening those who were sick and diseased. The shepherds of Israel let them lie in distress without binding up their broken bones. Furthermore, they did not seek the sheep that had been scattered and lost. They dominated them with force and severity (Ezek. 34:14). They became food for every beast of the field.

Here is Charles Spurgeon on not being kind to the depressed person:

> Remember what woes Ezekiel pronounces upon the strong that roughly push the weaker sort. God is very jealous over His little children, and if the more vigorous members of the family are not kind to them, He may take away their strength and make them, even, to envy the little ones whom once they despised. You can never err in being tender to the downcast. Lay yourself out as much as may be in you to bind up the brokenhearted and cheer the faint—and you will be blessed in the deed. When the natural spirits sink in those men who have no God to go to, their depression takes its own particular shape.[16]

The LORD told Israel that he would become their Shepherd. Before we look at Jesus as Shepherd, I would like to look at Isaiah's prophecy of the Lord Jesus Christ. As we have seen, Israel's leaders were called shepherds. The flock was first Israel and then the church of God. But now Isaiah brings in the Lord as a Shepherd who will tend His flock. Isaiah the prophet prophesied that God Himself would take charge of the sheep and be their shepherd. And he did so by sending His only begotten Son to become the God/Man Redeemer, Incarnate Deity. This prophecy was written about 739–681 BC. Isaiah 40:11 prophesizes about the Great Shepherd, God who became man:

> Like a shepherd He will tend His flock, in His arm He will gather the lambs and carry them in His bosom; He will gently lead the nursing ewes.

Jesus, the prophetic Shepherd, would be a gentle shepherd. Lambs are young sheep; they tire easily and must be gathered and carried. The word for "bosom" can also be used to refer to one who cherishes. Perhaps the shepherd wanted the lambs to hear his heartbeat. They are little and he protects them from harm and danger. If the sheep have no defense, then the lambs are all the more helpless. In the animal kingdom, predators always go after the young, easy prey. The ewes here are sucklings. Their mothers are their lifeline and without them these lambs would surely die.

Isaiah 40:11 has significant relevance for pastors shepherding the flock which God has given them. I believe an application to the mentally ill is appropriate, since some of the lambs could easily be in this category. Having a brain illness is one of the worse diagnoses known to man. The lot that has fallen to this portion of our society is extremely painful. It not only plagues the mind, but the whole body malfunctions. In a typical episode, people report a kind of roving pain, stomach problems, headache, and back pain. Other signs and symptoms vary, depending on the disorder. Mental illness symptoms can affect emotions, thoughts, and behaviors. Confusion, lack of concentration, excessive fears or guilt, mood changes, fatigue, gloomy or scary thoughts, unusual rituals, and detachment from reality are also common. To try to cope with this onslaught of symptoms alone or shepherd-less only adds to such a frightening situation.

There are people who label themselves biblical counselors but who still show a bias against those who have mental disorders. They may "play down" medications used to treat depression, bipolar disorder, panic disorder, etc. They teach that the Bible is the only remedy one needs when depressed, panicky, or suicidal. I call on my brothers to stop butting the sheep and hurting the lambs. Pastor, can you understand the love that the Triune God has for those who have mental illness? Do you understand that the Scripture said of our Lord Jesus?

> A bruised reed He will not break
> And a dimly burning wick He will not extinguish;
> He will faithfully bring forth justice (Isa. 42:3).

Our Lord Jesus is a wonderful shepherd. He said,

> Truly, truly, I say to you, I am the door of the sheep. All who came before Me are thieves and robbers, but the sheep did not hear them. I am the door; if anyone enters through Me, he will be saved, and will go in and out and find pasture. The thief comes only to steal and kill and destroy; I came that they may have life, and have it abundantly. I am the good shepherd; the good shepherd lays down His life for the sheep. He who is a hired hand, and not a shepherd, who is not the owner of the sheep, sees the wolf coming, and leaves the sheep and flees, and the wolf snatches them and scatters them (John 10:7–12).

Since our Lord Jesus was so compassionate toward suffering persons, why should we not be? He is the Good Shepherd.

Please help fight the stigma of mental illness in your church and among your pastor friends. We will have to give an account at the *bema* seat of how we ministered to people who are described as "smoking flax." They are God's lambs; they are his sucklings. These people need the true church to advocate for them and to protect them from predators, who want to maim and kill them.

A MAN CALLED PETER, SIMON PETER

Peter was a leader from the beginning. God called him to salvation, then to full-time ministry. Today's pastors are God's undershepherds, who must obey Peter's exhortation:

> Therefore, I exhort the elders among you, as your fellow elder and witness of the sufferings of Christ, and a partaker also of the glory that is to be revealed, shepherd the flock of God among you, exercising oversight not under compulsion, but voluntarily, according to the will of God; and not for sordid gain, but with eagerness; nor yet as lording it over those allotted to your charge, but proving to be examples to the flock. And when the Chief Shepherd appears, you will receive the unfading crown of glory (1 Peter 5:1–4).

The Restoration of Peter

God took Peter in the raw and we see him in the book of Acts boldly preaching. In First Peter we see a more mature, seasoned Peter, not caring whether he lived or died. He was filled with the Holy Spirit of God. Peter was a fisherman by trade. He had been taught to be a shepherd and a fisher of men by the Master Himself. The Bible tells us that after he denied Christ, during the arrest and trial of the Lord, he "wept bitterly." It appears later that he was considering leaving the ministry and going back to his fishing occupation. He felt unworthy to be a shepherd-pastor. But the Lord had different goals for him. He was going to restore Peter to a higher usefulness.

The story is found in John 21:15–17. "So when they had finished breakfast, Jesus said to Simon Peter, 'Simon, son of John, do you love Me more than these?'" The idea is that the Lord, speaking about "more than these," meant not the other disciples but the ship and all his fishing tackle. The Lord Jesus wanted to clearly show Peter that his work would not only be evangelistic but pastoral in nature. Peter answered him, "Yes, Lord; you know that I love you." Jesus said to him, "Tend My lambs." The word "tend" in the here is βοσκε.[17] It denotes more than just feeding; it entails guarding and some disciplining. In some sense, the lambs can mean those who are greatly tried. They are more weak than strong.

I know that when I was in the throes of depression, I was weaker than I had ever been, I needed extra care and I always appreciated it when a pastor was kind to me. On the contrary, Robyn and I get reports from all over the world telling us that their pastors "shame" those who are suffering from a mental illness.

The Lord Jesus said to Peter a second time:

> "Simon, son of John, do you love Me?" Peter said to Him, "Yes, Lord; You know that I love You." Jesus replied said to him, "Shepherd My sheep" (John 21:16).[18]

"He [then] said to him the third time, 'Simon, *son* of John, do you love Me?' Peter was grieved because He said to him the third time, 'Do you love Me?' And he said to Him, 'Lord, You know all things; You know that I love You.' Jesus said to him, 'Tend My sheep'" (John 21:17). In the Bible, when a phrase is repeated, it emphasizes the importance of what is said. It was also repeated three times as a reminder to Peter of his three denials. The Lord granted Peter a full pardon, and he did so in the presence of six other apostles so that no one would be able to say that the Lord had disqualified him. In fact, Christ gives him a charge that says the opposite in Luke 22:32b: "And you, when you have turned back, strengthen your brothers."[19]

In Peter's case recorded in Luke 22, part of his turning was from the sin of denying Christ. In my situation with biological depression, there was no sin from which to turn. My brain was assaulted by a substantiated clinical illness. I offer a quote from our book, *Broken Minds,* which relates an experience I had when I was being considered for a pastorate after my first episode:

> The senior pastor of our church suddenly called, confiding that he was about to resign and asking for Steve's help during the transition. He believed that Steve might well be the one to succeed him as pastor. When the search process began, Steve submitted his resume and awaited his pastoral interview. Some on the pulpit committee expressed concern about Steve's depression. These concerns were natural. What had his mental illness taken from Steve's qualifications as a pastor? What had God added to his abilities through his sickness? Looking back over two difficult years, it was obvious that a time could come when depression would make it impossible for Steve to fulfill his pastoral responsibilities. Someone might have to step in. There might be some feelings of embarrassment among the congregation if the pastor suddenly was unable to function because of mental illness. Pastors are supposed to be there for others with problems. They aren't supposed to have problems themselves. But a pastor diagnosed with depression could also offer some particular contributions.

> The interviews showed that a number of people felt that Steve's depression was a concern relating to the ministry. We contacted Charles Neff, Steve's Christian psychiatrist in Pennsylvania to ask for a professional assessment of Steve's illness and its effect on his ability to lead as a minister. The letter did not answer all the church's uncertainties, but what Dr. Neff said about Steve was an eloquent statement for what many depressed people can accomplish if allowed:

"... he is especially qualified having walked through a dark shadow of a valley which many people traverse who might well fall under his ministry, I feel he is a caring and earnest man who has great gifts and great strengths. I feel that the fact he has been wise enough to use appropriate treatment facilities is a great plus in his qualifications for any position of leadership in a church organization."[20]

About Peter, Charles Jefferson wrote.

When Jesus handed over to Simon Peter the charge of the Christian Church, he was careful to use the pronoun "my." "Feed my lambs! Tend my sheep! Feed my sheep!" It is the mightiest pronoun in the New Testament for the saving of the minister from lordliness. "Simon, son of Jonas, feed my lambs. They are not yours, they are mine, but I wish you to look after them for a little while. Tend my sheep. They are not yours. I do not give them to you. They belong to me. Mine they always shall remain, but I ask you to tend them for a season for me. Feed my sheep. They are not yours. Not one of them shall ever pass from my possession, but I am going away for a few days, and I leave them with you. Guard them, feed them, guide them, be good to them for my sake. Follow me. Remember my gentleness, my watchfulness, my considerateness, my patience, my compassion, my readiness to help, my swiftness to heal, my gladness to sacrifice. Be the kind of shepherd to my lambs and my sheep that I have been to you. Follow me!"[21]

NEEDED: PASTOR-SHEPHERDS

We need to have more pastors who shepherd God's flock, who minister in the spirit of the men of Issachar:

Now these are the numbers of the divisions equipped for war, who came to David at Hebron, to turn the kingdom of Saul to him, according to the word of the LORD. . . . Of the sons of Issachar, men who understood the times, with knowledge of what Israel should do (1 Chron. 12:23, 32).

Pastoral theology is a concept that there should be men in every generation who understand their generation and have the knowledge (the word of God) of what to do in those times. Ephesians 4 says that God gave pastor-teachers to equip the saints to do the work of the ministry. I believe that pastors need to be trained and train other believers in Christ, to help those who have mental illnesses and suffer from personality disorders.

First the pastor needs a solid systematic and biblical theology. He should be like Ezra, of whom we read:

For on the first of the first month he began to go up from Babylon; and on the first of the fifth month he came to Jerusalem, because the good hand of his God was upon him. For Ezra had set his heart to study the law of the LORD and to practice it, and to teach His statutes and ordinances in Israel (Ezra 7:9–10).

Secondly, this idea of mental illness in the church is not a marginal problem. Far too many pastors are either uneducated about mental health issues or erroneously taught that the Bible is all a person needs to deal with their illness. We would not say that about a heart problem, Alzheimer's disease, or a dermatological issue. However, when a disease affects a person's mood, thinking, and behavior the issue becomes blurred. After a pastor has a solid foundation of Scripture, he should get further training in dealing with mental illness.

Call for Pastoral Counseling

When I was first saved, our church had a counseling pastor who was very helpful. Today, one can scarcely find a "pastor of counseling." There are two reasons for this. One is that the evangelical church has dropped the pastor of counseling and has replaced him with family ministries. Do we really need a pastor for every age group? Another is that mental health professionals have replaced counseling/shepherding pastors. The problem with this is that mental health professionals, for the most part, are not pastors or even believers. I would like to see the counseling pastor reinstated. One of his important tasks would be to help minister to the mentally ill.

A good pastor-shepherd will lead his people through preaching, discipleship, and counseling. When they are fearful, his rod and his staff will comfort him. When they are agitated and nervous, he will calm them. When they are hungry and weak, he will find them good pasture. He will show them a more excellent way, which is to have *agape* love—as elucidated in 1 Corinthians 13 by the apostle Paul, who was one of the greatest pastors of all time. Was Paul a preacher? Yes. Was he a theologian? Yes. Was he an exhorter? Yes! Remember, he is the one who said to the Thessalonian church, "admonish the unruly, encourage the fainthearted" (1 Thess. 5:14).

This encouraging of tottering, trembling believers is very biblical. In the previous Scripture, the word "encourage"[22] in the original language (Greek) is a compound word which means "to get close to a person in a very friendly manner and offer them consolation, using Scripture narratives to provide healing of the soul." The word "fainthearted" is the Greek term *oligo psuchos*, which literally means "small-souled." The minds of mentally ill people are subject to great weakness. They possess a fractured mind, and the result is very little inner resource. This is reflected in Proverbs 18:14, "The spirit of a man can endure his sickness, but as for a broken spirit who can bear it?"[23]

It cannot be emphasized enough that support groups for the mentally ill, done in the right fashion, will help accomplish the strengthening and edification of the mentally ill and their families. As a shepherd, God's man can give great comfort and teach others do so. Why is it tempting at times to *warn* the fainthearted and *encourage* the unruly instead of warn the *unruly* and encourage the *fainthearted*? Is it because we are afraid to confront the unruly in light of their possible reaction, whereas the weak do not have the strength to fight back? When we accuse the fainthearted of being in sin (i.e., having depression), they cannot explain or defend themselves; they are too weak. As Charles Jefferson says, in his magnificent book *The Minister as Shepherd*:

> Many a minister fails as a pastor because he is not vigilant. He allows his church to be torn to pieces because he is half asleep. He took it for granted that there were no wolves, no birds of prey, and no robbers and while he was drowsy the enemy arrived. False ideas, destructive interpretations, demoralizing teachings came into his group, and he never knew it. He was interested, perhaps in literary research; he was absorbed in the discussion contained in the last theological quarterly, and did not know what his young people were reading, or what strange ideas had been lodged in the heads of a group of his leading members. There are errors which are as fierce as wolves and pitiless as hyenas; they tear faith and hope and love to pieces and leave their churches, once prosperous, mangled and half dead.[24]

Right before my first depression in 1985, I did not realize that anything was wrong with me. While there had to be the seeds of depression in my mind and body, I was still feeling fine. I was preparing for a trip to Buffalo, New York, in March and the weather report was not good. Robyn was a little worried and I remember saying to her, "A man is immortal until his work on earth is through." What I said was true but in my life it had not yet been tested.

I had just been ordained and was feeling as Adoniram Judson did when he said, "The Future is as bright as the Promises of God."[25] I really had no notion of the horror of darkness and depression that would paralyze and assault me; and it was just around the corner. No matter how a person tries to describe major depression, it is unfathomable suffering. If you have experienced the darkness of the soul, you know exactly what I am talking about. Many Bible characters knew this terror. For instance when Abram was participating in the ceremony of the Abrahamic covenant it was said:

> The birds of prey came down upon the carcasses, and Abram drove them away. Now when the sun was going down, a deep sleep fell upon Abram; and behold, terror and great darkness fell upon him, God said to Abram, "Know for certain that your descendants will be strangers in a land that is not theirs, where they will be enslaved and oppressed four hundred years"(Gen. 15:11–13).

The word for terror in the above passage is used for that state of mind that the LORD had put on the Canaanites as they faced annihilation from Joshua and the Hebrew armies, whose captain was the LORD of Hosts. Rahab the harlot hid the Israeli spies, and said to the men:

> I know that the LORD has given you the land, and that the *terror*[26] of you has fallen on us, and that all the inhabitants of the land have melted away before you (Josh. 2:8–9, emphasis added).

The word for *darkness*[27] is used to describe Abraham's mood after the LORD sedated him with a deep sleep. The darkness was temporary but nightmarish. David, the shepherd of Israel, used a word for darkness when he talked about "the valley of the shadow of death" (Ps. 23:4). The Hebrew word for "shadow of death" is *tsalmaveth,* or "black gloom."[28] Jeremiah 13:16 is another example of this: "Give glory to the LORD your God, before He brings darkness, and before your feet stumble on the dusky mountains. And while you are hoping for light He makes it into deep darkness, and turns it into gloom."

If you are a pastor-shepherd, do you know the people in your church who are struggling right now with depression? It is called "the common cold of mental illness." They are there: in your services, in your small groups, and in your counseling sessions. They might not present themselves as being depressed. They would more likely say they cannot sleep, do not have an appetite, and are continually stressed out to the point of having problems at work or at home.[29]

Many people have talked about Spurgeon's depression and the reason he had it. One of the important details that made his preaching effective is his own transparency. He understood the souls of men and women who experienced darkness and did not berate them for it. Below is an abridged version his powerful sermon, "A Child of Light, Walking in Darkness."

> Who is among you that fears the Lord? The same God who also spies out His children in the dark, and looking upon them with an eye of tender love, He directs their course. This is the word of wisdom by which He directs each one of them through the darkness, "Let Him trust in the name of the Lord, and stay upon his God."
>
> O you, who are walking in the light, deal gently with your Brothers and Sisters whose bones are broken, for you may also suffer from the same! Lay yourselves out to comfort the Lord's mourners. They are not good company and they are very apt to make you unhappy as well as themselves, but for all that, be very tender towards them, for the Lord Jesus would have you so. Those of you who are always bright need not be afraid of your gladness.
>
> O Lord! We are now and then in the dark, but we do not wish others to be so. Spiritual darkness of any sort is to be avoided, and not desired, and yet, surprising as it may seem to be, it is a fact that some of the best of God's people frequently walk in darkness; yes, some of them are wrapped in a sevenfold gloom at times, and to them neither sun, nor moon, nor stars appear.
>
> As the pastor of a large church, I have to observe a great variety of experiences, and I note that some whom I greatly love and esteem, who are, in my judgment among the very choicest of God's people, nevertheless, travel most of the way to heaven by night. They do not rejoice in the light of God's countenance,

though they trust in the shadow of His wings. They are on the way to eternal light, and yet they walk in darkness.

When first brought home to the great Father, we thought that henceforth it would be all music and dancing and fatted calf, world without end. But it is not so; we have heard the elder brother's un-generous voice since then, and we have found out many things which we wish we could forget. We dreamed that the year would be summer throughout all its months; the time of the singing of birds was come, and we reckoned that it was to continue through the year. Alas! The birds have ceased their songs, and the swallows are pluming their wings to depart, and in a few days we shall be walking among the falling leaves, and preparing our winter garments with which to meet the biting frosts. We have not found perfect bliss beneath the moon. Be not, therefore, surprised as though some strange thing had happened unto you, if you find yourself in darkness, for this text warns you of what you may expect. We may fear God and carefully obey His servant, and yet we may be out after dark and find the streets of daily life as foggy and obscure for us as for others. This condition is a severe test of grace. Now we shall see how far the man's courage is of the right sort. Darkness is an evil that our soul does not love, and by it all our faculties are tried. If you are in your own house in the dark it does not matter, though children do not like to be put to bed in the dark even in their own little room, but if you are on a journey and you come to a wild moor, or a vast forest, or to terrible mountains, it appalls you to find that the sun is setting, and that you will be abroad in the dark.

Darkness has a terrible power of causing fear; its mystery is an influence creating dread. It is not what we see that we dread, as much as that which we do not see, and therefore exaggerate. When darkness lowers down upon the believer's mind it is a great trial to his heart. He cries, "Where am I? And how did I come here? If I am a child of God, why am I thus? Did I really repent and obtain light so as to escape the darkness of sin? If so, why am I conscious of this thick gloom? Did I really joy in Christ and think I had received the atonement? Why, then, has the sun of my joy gone down so hopelessly? Where are now the loving-kindnesses of the Lord?"

The good man begins to question himself as to every point of his profession, for in the dark he cannot even judge his own self. What is worse, he sometimes questions the truth which he has before received, and doubts the very ground on which his feet are resting. Satan will come in with vile insinuations questioning everything, even as he questioned God's Word when he ruined our race in the garden. It is possible at such times even to question the existence of the God we love, though we still cling to Him with desperate resolve. We undergo a life and death struggle while we hold on to the divine verities. We are at times sorely put to it, and scarcely know what to do. Like the mariners with whom Paul sailed, we cast four anchors out of the stern, and look for the day. Oh, that we could be certain that we are the Lord's! Oh, that we could apprehend the sure promises of the Lord, and our portion in them! For a while the darkness is all around us, and we perceive no candle of the Lord, or spark of experimental light with which to break the gloom. This darkness is very trying to faith, trying to love, trying to hope, trying to patience, trying to every grace of the spiritual man. Blessed is the man who can endure this test.[30]

In the New Testament, we see clearly that the Lord Jesus Christ is the Good Shepherd:

> I am the good shepherd; the good shepherd lays down His life for the sheep. He who is a hired hand, and not a shepherd, who is not the owner of the sheep, sees the wolf coming, and leaves the sheep and flees, and the wolf snatches them and scatters them. He flees because he is a hired hand and is not concerned about the sheep. I am the good shepherd, and I know My own and My own know Me (John 10:11–14).

This is fairly early in Jesus' ministry; already He is talking about the blood atonement that He, the Good Shepherd, will give for His sheep. He is not only the Good Shepherd; it was said by John the Baptist, "Behold, the Lamb of God which takes away the sin of the world!" (John 1:29). Isaiah also tells us:

> He was oppressed and He was afflicted, yet He did not open His mouth; Like a lamb that is led to slaughter, and like a sheep that is silent before its shearers, so He did not open His mouth (Isa. 53:7).

If we want to be good shepherds, we must prayerfully represent our Lord as He is revealed in the Word of God. He is our great example. Thankfully, we have the Spirit of Christ in us. We have access to the power of God in our ongoing sanctification. One of your tasks as pastor is to help the church proclaim and testify about this amazing Shepherd, the God-Man who gave his life for the sins of the world.

Part of being obedient to the Lord is to take His word and teach it to the saints. It is often overlooked, but there are implicit and explicit commands regarding those who are mentally ill. Consider this passage which talks about Christ in Matthew 12:20 (KJV): "A bruised reed shall He not break, and smoking flax shall he not quench, till He send forth judgment unto victory." These are descriptions about the children of God who have been crushed emotionally and are at the end of their only resources. God does not come to them in their fragile, unstable state as a harsh disciplinarian, but as Shepherd who is there to carry them—to sustain the bruised reed and to fan the flame of that dim and flickering candle.

Have an attitude of compassion. If you have no compassion for the mentally ill, then please stay out of their way. They have a crushed spirit and there are many Scriptures that instruct us to be caring and compassionate with weakened people such as these. If you are a pastor, then you are directly exhorted biblically to help the suffering sheep. I have been treated with disdain by pastors and church members. It is very demoralizing, and if it happens while I am in an episode of depression, it is like an officer in war shooting his own wounded soldier. There still are many "biblical counselors" who are not really biblical in their approach. They believe in a one-size-fits-all approach to helping a depressed person. The Bible is not a book that teaches such an easy treatment. People who trouble the mentally ill are like a hacker's virus which upsets the highly tuned computer, wreaking havoc on its system. Much of my ministry has been acting like effective antivirus software. It involves detecting the people who do not have compassion, and eliminating the damaging effect of the virus.

Paul gathered before him the elders from Ephesus. He tells them they were made overseers of a flock of God because the God/Man by his shed blood purchased them and the flock they were called to pastor. We have mentioned Peter and his restoration to ministry. Now we go to the first of two epistles that he wrote:

> Therefore I exhort the elders among you, as your fellow elder and witness of the sufferings of Christ, and a partaker also of the glory that is to be revealed, shepherd the flock of God among you, exercising oversight not under compulsion, but voluntarily according to the will of God; and not for sordid gain but with eagerness; nor yet as lording it over those allotted to your charge, but proving to be examples to the flock. And when the chief Shepherd appears you will receive the unfading crown of glory (1 Peter 5:1–4).

Peter had suffered after Christ was raised, eventually to be crucified upside-down on a cross. He was a much bolder preacher, and man, after his restoration:

> AND IF IT IS WITH DIFFICULTY THAT THE RIGHTEOUS IS SAVED, WHAT WILL BECOME OF THE GODLESS MAN AND THE SINNER? Therefore, those also who suffer according to the will of God shall entrust their souls to a faithful Creator in doing what is right (1 Peter 4:18–19).

In order to effectively minister to the sheep in your flock, let them be aware of some of your own difficulties. I have found people relate much better to me in my struggles than in my successes. Remember what Paul said: He learned when he was weak that he was strong (2 Cor. 12:10). Pastors who deny the existence of mental illness show that they don't understand how vulnerable anyone is to a brain disorder. Many pastors have become much more understanding and empathetic about depression when their wives or children are suddenly stricken. I did not believe it myself until it hit me in 1985. The pain and disruption of my life were monumental and life-changing.

DEPRESSION AND JESUS CHRIST THE SON OF GOD

While I was at a recent speaking engagement, I mentioned that the Lord Jesus Christ was depressed in the Garden of Gethsemane. Some people were offended by this. When God wants to prepare a pastor, he trains him by giving him trials so that he can identify with those who suffer. In fact, the same type of preparation (except without sin or pre-cross chastisement) happened to our Lord Jesus. Our Lord was a man of sorrows. The writer of Hebrews tells us:

> In the days of His flesh, He offered up both prayers and supplications with loud crying and tears to the One able to save Him from death, and He was heard because of His piety. Although He was a Son, He learned obedience from the things which He suffered. And having been made perfect, He became to all those who obey Him the source of eternal salvation (Heb. 5:7–9).

It is important to reflect on the doctrine of the hypostatic union. The hypostatic union is the term used to describe how God the Son took on a human nature, yet remained fully God (John 1:14). The addition of the human nature to the divine nature is Jesus, the God-Man. Jesus, through his human nature, did have tears for his own grief. This was not selfish; he was a man and he was God. But he had the joy set before Him:

> [F]ixing our eyes on Jesus, the author and perfecter of our faith, who for the joy set before Him endured the cross, despising the shame, and has sat down at the right hand of the throne of God (Heb. 12:2).

Think about how Jesus now has firsthand experience of intense depression, as He intercedes before the Father for us in our weakness. Three passages that record Jesus' experience in the garden are Mark 14 and Matthew 26 and Luke 22.

Mark 14:33 (KJV) relates: "And he taketh with him Peter and James and John, and began to be sore amazed, and to be very heavy." One of the two Greek verbs used is εκτηαμβειστηαι, from εκτηαμβεομαι, which means "to be amazed; alarmed; greatly astonished." The other is αδεμονειν, from αδεμονεο, meaning "to be troubled or intensely depressed and distressed."

Matthew 26:37–38 says:

> And He took with Him Peter and the two sons of Zebedee, and began to be grieved and distressed. Then He said to them, "My soul is deeply grieved, to the point of death; remain here and keep watch with Me."

In verse 37, the word αδεμονειν is used alongside λψπειστηαι, from λψπεο, meaning "to grieve; weep; be sad or depressed." In verse 38 Jesus says, "My soul is deeply grieved, to the point of death." "Deeply grieved" is from περιλψποσ, combining the preposition περι, meaning "around," with λῦπσ, meaning "sad." The sadness is intense, as one surrounded by sorrow. Here Jesus says that He is near death with sorrow. It was after this that an angel appeared to strengthen Him (Luke 22:43; c.f. Matt. 4:11).

In Luke 22:44, "and being in agony He was praying very fervently;" the words "and being in agony" are from the Greek εν αγονια. In classic Greek literature, the αγον was a place of a great contest. It came to refer to a contest, race, struggle, or fight. The most intense words available to refer to emotions and emotional states were used to describe Christ's struggle at Gethsemane. Charles Gabriel, the author of the hymn "My Savior's Love" in 1905, wrote inaccurately, "He had no tears for his own grief but sweat drops of blood for mine." Jesus Christ was preparing to take the wrath of God for our sins. The Father would charge those offenses to Christ for punishment. God would forsake Jesus, leaving Him in the lurch. For Jesus, the agony was so horrible that in utter darkness on the cross, He cried, "My God, My God, Why have you forsaken me?" On the cross, He does not use the affectionate word of a child for a father, "Abba." He spoke as the "one mediator . . . between God and men, the man Christ Jesus, who gave Himself as a ransom for all, the testimony given at the proper time" (1 Timothy 2:5–6).

In his exposition of Psalm 40, Spurgeon says,

> When our Lord bore in His own person the terrible curse which was due sin, He was so cast down as to be like a prisoner in a deep, dark, fearful dungeon, amid whose horrible glooms the captive heard a noise as of rushing torrents, while overhead resounded the tramp of furious foes. Our Lord in His anguish was like a captive in the oubliettes [dungeon with an opening only at the top], forgotten of all mankind, immured amid horror, darkness, and desolation. Yea the Lord Jehovah made Him to ascend from all His abasement. He retraced His steps from that deep hell of anguish into which He had been cast as our substitute. He, who thus delivered our surety in extremis, will not fail to liberate us from our lighter grieves.[31]

A fourth aspect of a good pastoral theology is that which recognizes diversity of the schemes of the devil and his demons to derail the Christian and an explanation how to resist the attacks. There needs to be an explanation of the wiles of the devil and how to resist him. The question is, "Does the devil use his devices against those who are suffering from mental illness?" Yes, he does, and we need to anticipate his attacks. The devil loves to take advantage of us in our weakness. He doesn't back away because we are having enough problems. If you are in great grief, emotionally weak, or sick with a bodily illness, Satan and his demons are not gentlemen. He constantly looks for an opportune time. He wants you for dinner. Remember, he is the Evil One, the prince of the power of air, the prince of darkness, a liar, and a slanderer.

His demons seek to overwhelm those who are believers in Christ with sorrow, fears, and doubts, even to the point where you feel God has given up on you. He wants you isolated, alone with nowhere to turn. Christ soundly defeated him on the cross and he will burn forever in the lake of fire, but he is still in the world today tempting believers to sin. When a person is already dealing with mental illness, the fight can be more difficult. But it is doable! We never have an excuse to say that the temptation was too great and that we could not help but sin (1 Cor. 10:13; 2 Cor. 1:8–11). Our great Savior will empower us to resist sin, but if our friends do not understand and our Christian leaders are not accurately informed, we are pushed to suffer in silence. If ever the church is needed, it is in this situation. Prayer is necessary, should be encouraged, and we should not be embarrassed to ask for it. Since the beginning of time, Satan has been devouring believers.

In order to develop a biblical theology of the devil and his aims and methods, we must go to the Bible. How do you fight the devil's attacks to bring you down? He must be resisted by the child of God, as James tells us in James 4:7, "Submit therefore to God. Resist the devil and he will flee from you." Note the order; you cannot resist the devil unless you first submit to God. In your own strength and sinfulness, you will soon be conquered.

The great Puritan theologian John Owen had something to say about the church fighting evil:

> The gates of hell, as all agree are the power and policy of it, or the acting's of Satan, both as a lion and as a serpent, by rage and by subtlety. He does not act in a visible manner, in his own person, but by his agents. He always has two sorts of them that work for him. He uses one class of demons and through them carries out his intention, which is his rage, and by the other his craft; which is his seductions; he now is acting like a lion and then acting like a serpent. The Satanic work of this kind is of a double nature;—the one, an effect of his power and rage, acted by the world in persecution—the other, of his policy and craft, acted by heretics in seduction.[32]

The devil's plan was to tempt and deceive the Corinthians that they should be over-tolerant toward the man who had been immoral with his father's wife. The church took the bait and ran with it (1 Cor. 5; 2 Cor. 2:6–11). One of the things the Bible teaches is that the devil is able to attack us by way of the mind. Like any general, he uses his officers (demons) to plan strategic attacks on nations, families, and individuals. The Bible also calls these methods "thoughts." The use of thoughts is seen in 2 Corinthians 2 where the apostle Paul tells us we must not be ignorant of his schemes. The word *noma* for "schemes" here means a mental perception, thought, and an evil purpose. It has to do with the mind formulating and organizing plans. Then there are purposes,[33] and this of course implies a battle plan which is then carried out, skillfully, for every believer. So in a general sense we must understand these powerful, deceiving beings that are wreaking havoc on the people of God. Corinth was known for its open immorality, with temple prostitutes and all kinds of other fornication and sexual deviancy. And it was quite easy for the church to accept the young man's sexual transgression. But Paul wrote them and told them to discipline the adulterer and put him out of the church (see the whole chapter of 1 Corinthians 5). The church obeyed the Lord and disciplined the offender.

Next the devil tempted the church to be unforgiving by not letting the repentant man back into the fellowship. The devil sought by this whole incident to gain an advantage over the church and the man who was disciplined. Robertson says, "that no advantage may be gained over us." Paul writes and tells them to comfort him.

The devil then tempted the repentant stepson to despair because he found himself in no man's land between the church and the world. Satan's scheme with this attack, which he and his minions have no doubt further perfected in time, seeks to alienate the Christian from a sense of peace and love. Another one of Satan's names used in the Bible is "devil," which means slanderer. This term coupled with Satan, which means adversary, demonstrates who he is, as all of Scripture shows him as a merciless accuser of the brethren.

A principle seen here is that the devil seeks to demoralize Christians and "swallow them up." I would like to make an observation of how the devil can use the church to alienate and overwhelm people who have a mental illness. The reason would not be the same as the sinning brother in 1 Corinthians, but the result can be similar. People with mental illness in our churches are often met with a critical spirit from those who should be embracing them. They feel sorrow from the disease itself, and then the rejection or criticism from their Christian brothers and sisters drives them to total despair. We need to love and care for the hurting, and stop blaming them for something that is an illness and not moral failure.

Paul says, "Sufficient for such a one is this punishment which was inflicted by the majority, so that on the contrary you should rather forgive and comfort him, otherwise such a one might be overwhelmed[34] by excessive sorrow" (2 Cor. 2:6–7). Satan was using the unforgiving spirit of the Corinthian church working through its members to alienate and destroy him, but God in his mercy caused the church to admit him back into the fellowship.

In 1 and 2 Peter, the apostle shepherded the people with a great fervor. In 1 Peter, he also used the Greek word καταπινο, which is translated "overwhelmed." It is also the same Greek word that was used earlier in the case of the Corinthian offender. Peter tells us,

> Therefore humble yourselves under the mighty hand of God, that He may exalt you at the proper time, casting all your anxiety on Him, because He cares for you. Be of sober spirit, be on the alert. Your adversary, the devil, prowls around like a roaring lion, seeking someone to devour. But resist him, firm in your faith, knowing that the same experiences of suffering are being accomplished by your brethren who are in the world (1 Peter 5:6–9).

So then we see that God has made provision for us to not be conquered by the devil when it comes to our intellect, emotions, and will. These areas of the mind, mood, and volition are greatly affected by mental illness and so we would expect that dragon to attack those spheres. Peter had learned from his previous sifting by Satan (see Luke 24) that one must be humble and alert. He had bought into the devil's plan for him to deny Christ, and it almost cost him his ministry. But God is the God of second chances. Peter also talks about anxiety and how you should cast it on the Lord. If you have an anxiety disorder, doing this will be more difficult. You must remember this is a command of love, not of the law. You do the best you can and God expects no more. Peter also states that you must be of sober[35] spirit and on the alert. Again Peter no doubt remembered how he was filled with pride before he denied Christ and slept from sorrow. Our Lord told him to watch and to pray. Peter failed to do so. Therefore the devil attempted to devour or swallow him up (καταπινο).

The order for battle is: First, you must be strong in the strength of the Lord, and the power of his might; secondly, you must put on the full armor of God. In Ephesians 6:11, Paul writes; "put on the full armor of God, so that you will be able to stand firm against the schemes of the devil." The Greek word for "schemes" here is μεΤηοδια. If you are a Christian, you cannot retreat from spiritual battles. The Roman soldier had no armor for the back. The demons of hell will not relent. The enemy will not just leave. He has come to fight you, soldier of the light. We need to put on the armor of God. We should not be ignorant of Satan's schemes. He may leave, then, and come back at another time. The Christian soldier can only put down his sword and take off his armor when he dies, or when Christ comes back to "catch up" the true church at His coming.

People under the stress of mental illness could be said to be in the fog of war, where confusion abounds and the ability to stay the course at times seems almost beyond human ability to cope. This, of course, would depend on what kind of mental illness the person has. We must oppose the devil and stand against him. We do not want an advantage taken of us by Satan. His wish is to drive us into despair. He wants to demoralize us. The wiles of the devil are universal, but for our purposes we are going to focus our attention toward the mentally ill and spiritual warfare.

GOD IS NOT MAD AT YOU!

Realize that though you may not feel His presence, the Lord is concerned about every hair on your head. He also cares about the millions of neurons which are not firing in your brain. This mental anguish that you feel is real. It is not your fault. God is not mad at you, and there are treatments to help you.

Realize that you must resist suicide, and get help for your mental illness.

The devil creates confusion between the physical, psychological, and spiritual realms.[36] This is an effective device of the devil. A person with mental illness might be referred to a psychologist or a certain therapist, who will say to him, "You really need extensive therapy for your negative outlook and depression." The person with mental illness becomes confused. He goes to therapy and spends a considerable amount of money—but he remains depressed, and can't sleep at night. Some medical doctor may have seen him and told him he needed a sleeping pill. The obvious problem is that he has a mental illness, probably major depression with comorbidity of panic disorder.

If we don't realize it is physical, then we search for a psychological or spiritual cure. Some professionals still insist depression is one-third spiritual, one-third physical, and one-third psychological. How overly simplistic! Has anyone ever had his life neatly divided into thirds like this? There may be an element of truth to the crossover of symptoms or borderline cases. But if a person has a mental illness that responds to a psychotropic medication, the other areas generally take care of themselves. This is a very important scheme of the devil. His accusations are so serious in this realm that believing brothers and sisters think they are missing some spiritual secret because their brains are not performing correctly. They blame themselves for a lack of spirituality, refuse medications, become so despondent and muddled in their thinking, that the end is death—their own death at their own hands. The devil is a liar and a murderer, and he takes every advantage he can to take precious lives.

The person who is suffering from mental illness first must get over the stigma of going to a psychiatrist. He or she must realize they are physicians who treat the brain. The patient should be willing to take medication. It should be an antidepressant; or if a person has bipolar disease, she should take a mood stabilizer. These pills do no harm, but are very effective in treating mental illness. It is not a spiritual problem, not a psychological problem, but a medical problem. Many people, when they are having (for lack of a better term) a "break," will actually come to the pastor for help. At this time you, as a pastor, must be a physician of souls.

The devil wants to confuse the difference between temptation and sin. This is an especially effective strategy against a Christian with obsessive compulsive disorder (OCD). How does the pastor help the sufferer to distinguish the difference between temptation to sin and an obsession? All of us have to deal with thoughts that are sinful and even blasphemous. There is a difference, of course, between the temptation to sin and the actual act of sinning (James 1:13–17), yet we also know that thoughts can be sinful when we accept and act on them. The common saying is helpful, "You can't stop a bird from flying over your head, but you can stop him from building a nest." The difference is a conundrum for people who have Obsessive Compulsive Disorder.

I was very depressed, but still between a severe and moderate episode of depression. I also was having OCD symptoms. One of my most frequent obsessions was an inability to believe with assurance that the veil in the temple was torn in two from top to bottom as the Scripture says. When I was prescribed the right medication, I no longer had the obsession. Some obsessions are more difficult and debilitating than my example. For these people we would use cognitive behavioral therapy plus medication to alleviate the symptoms.

A good pastoral theology, then, affects the care and maintenance of your flock.
We must have a thorough understanding of Scripture and know how to apply the principles that are found there. We are not called to be Bible answer men, but shepherds.

Community Resources for Pastors
When we talk about community resources, it boils down to three different ways of accessing helpers. Some will come from the church, some from the community, and others from medical and social work interventions.

The church that I am referencing is the individual local entity of evangelical believers, which include the pastor, deacons, and the membership. This book is written for one of the most important characters in the church and that is her pastor. Pastors can also be called shepherds; the same Greek word, ποιμεν, is translated "pastor" in Ephesians 4:11 and "shepherd" in 1 Peter 5:2. In the chapter on shepherds, I give an extensive account of the pastor-shepherd. You may want to read that section a couple of times. As a pastor, you have been prepared by God for your ministry as you teach and preach the word of God to your congregation.

As a shepherd, you counsel sheep in your church on a regular basis. Some of those who need help are those suffering with mental illness, or may be family members who support them. Since you are reading this book, you have an obvious interest in assisting those with mental health issues. You are seeking ways to counsel and guide them. We trust this book will guide you in the right direction.

People who have depression disorder, bipolar disorder, panic disorder, OCD, or any of the other mental disorders are filling your churches. I wonder sometimes if the church depends too much on the government to step in where the church should already be standing. In some churches, the benevolence fund should be a larger portion of the church's overall budget. A mentally ill person desperately needs medicine, and sometimes medications are just unaffordable. I also urge young people who are going into the medical field to consider psychiatry or another mental health discipline. Knowledgeable, caring Christians are a blessing to those who are hurting.

I offer pastors special training through Heartfelt Counseling Ministries. My theological education and my social work background have given me a unique perspective. You won't become a "licensed counselor" unless you go back to college for that purpose, but you will be trained thoroughly in what to do with people who are desperate for direction. Your deacons and other pastoral staff can also be trained through our CAMI program. We hold training sessions to learn how to start a support group for the mentally ill in your church.

Another good way for a church to have an impact on the mentally ill is to enlist volunteers among its members and friends. In the United States, we need to know how to avail ourselves of county, state, and federal programs. When we live and work in our state, we pay taxes. Part of those taxes goes toward funding the effective treatment of mental illness. The federal government also funds these programs. As pastors, we should know what is offered.

Are you aware of the community mental health centers near you and your church? These centers serve people who do not have the money or insurance coverage to get the treatment they need. The mentally ill can also call the local United Way. In most states, you need to only dial 2–1–1, or go to their website (www.referweb.net/211community resources) and enter your zip code. The United Way provides free booklets that explain how to access health care which, naturally, includes mental health. If you have access to the Internet, a Google search is all you need to find appropriate services.

Your members, as believers, may feel more comfortable with a counselor who knows Christ as Savior and has a good understanding of the Bible. There are specific forms of psychotherapy that have been shown to be helpful for mild to moderate depression, such as cognitive behavior therapy or cognitive therapy. Many therapists use a mix of styles.

It is helpful if a therapist is compassionate and understanding regarding the pain of mental illness. Peer support groups are becoming more popular, because no one understands the suffering of mental illness like another person who has suffered mental illness. It is therapeutic in itself to be comforted and directed by a "wounded healer." Pastors who have "been there" make good counselors, especially if they have had adequate training.

What if treatment doesn't help? Once you've settled on a therapist and a doctor, your role becomes that of a coach helping your counselee persevere through the psychic pain until the therapy and medication begin to work. Getting better takes time, often several months. Treatment for depression can be exhausting at first. Opening up to someone about very personal things in one's life isn't easy. The medication itself can take at least ten days to even begin to have its effect and months to feel the full effect. The patient needs supportive therapy during these early weeks.

I close this introduction with the words of Charles Jefferson:

> It is the mission of a pastor to minister to minds diseased; to pluck from the memory a rooted sorrow; to raze out the written troubles of the brain; and with some oblivious antidote, to cleanse the stuffed bosom of that perilous stuff, which weighs upon the heart. There is always someone ailing in the parish, not physically only, but mentally, morally, spirituality. The diseases of the soul are numerous, and the remedies provided by the Almighty are efficacious only when applied by a skilled physician.
>
> There are soul diseases peculiar to certain ages and certain temperaments, and certain callings and certain environments; the minister ought to know

the symptoms of these diseases, the stages of development, and the hygienic processes by which they may be cured. . . . Here is a field in which the minister is called upon to put forth his skill and strength. His mission is to the sick, and all sick people are not sick with the same sickness, nor do they require the same remedies or the same kind of nursing.[37]

THE CAST OF CHARACTERS IN A MENTAL HEALTH CRISIS

TO WHOM DO I GO?

Adult Nurse Practitioner (ANP)/Certified Nurse Practitioner (NP-C)
Adult nurse practitioners are registered nurses who serve as primary and specialty health care providers under a physician. Much like a family doctor, family nurse practitioners work with patients throughout their lives, diagnosing illnesses, conducting exams, and prescribing medications. Nurse practitioners are advanced registered nurses educated and trained to provide health promotion and maintenance through the diagnosis and treatment of acute illness and chronic conditions.

Developmental/Behavioral Pediatricians
Developmental and behavioral pediatricians are pediatric subspecialists who have completed two additional years of training in evaluating and treating developmental and behavioral problems, and hence may offer both more expertise and more experience than a general pediatrician when it comes to children with developmental disorders, though they may not have training in psychiatry and expertise in psychotropic medications.[38]

Licensed Clinical Social Worker (LCSW)/ Clinical Social Workers
Typically a clinical social worker will have completed a master's degree in social work (M.S.W.), and will carry the LCSW designation if doing psychotherapy. Most programs require the professional to go through thousands of hours of direct clinical experience, and the program focuses on teaching principles of psychotherapy and social work.

Marriage and Family Therapist (MFT)
These therapists tend to have a master's degree (this varies by the professional's age and whether they live in California, where a master's degree is not required), and typically have between hundreds to thousands of hours of direct clinical experience. Because this designation varies from state to state, the quality of the professional may also vary significantly from person to person.

Medical Doctor (MD or DO)

An MD is a medical doctor, and a DO is an osteopathic physician. Both are licensed physicians who will oversee your care. These are usually primary care physicians who order blood work and tests, and make referals to specialists. They are on call for medical emergencies. They can prescribe medications that help mental illness; and if you need further care they will be the ones to refer you to a psychiatrist.

Mental Health Professional (MHP)

A mental health professional is a health care practitioner or community services provider who offers services for the purpose of improving an individual's mental health or to treat mental illness. This broad category was developed as a name for community personnel who worked in community mental health agencies, which began in the 1970s to assist individuals moving from state hospitals, to prevent admissions, and to provide support in homes, jobs, education, and community. These individuals were in the forefront of developing the community programs, which today include supported housing, psychiatric rehabilitation, supported or transitional employment, sheltered workshops, supported education, daily living skills, affirmative industries, dual diagnosis treatment, individual and family psychoeducation, adult day care, foster care, family services, and mental health counseling.

Neurologist

A neurologist is a medical doctor who specializes in disorders of the nervous system—which, of course, includes the brain. Neurologists can identify nervous system causes of some worrying symptoms and aid in the treatment of neurological and neurodevelopmental disorders, including cerebral palsy and epilepsy.

Pediatric Neurologist

Pediatric neurologists complete five years of training and clinical experience in pediatrics and pediatric neurology after medical school. They specialize in the treatment of neurodevelopmental disorders, including intellectual disability, Tourette's, ADHD, and learning disabilities.[39]

Pediatric Psychiatric Nurse Practitioner

Nurse practitioners have advanced degrees, either a master's or a doctorate, and can prescribe medication. A *pediatric psychiatric* nurse practitioner has training in treating and monitoring children and adolescents with psychiatric disorders. Some work as part of a team in a pediatricians' office; some practice independently.

Primary Care Provider

Primary care providers—such as internists, pediatricians, and family physicians—may provide initial components of mental health diagnosis and treatment for children and adults; however, family physicians in some states refuse to even prescribe a psychotropic medication, deferring to separately funded "medication management" services. Community programs in the categorical field of mental health were designed in the 1970s to have a personal family physician for every client in their programs, except for institutional settings and nursing facilities which have only one or two for a large facility.

Psychiatric Nurse
Psychiatric nurses are trained first as a regular registered nurses (RNs), but get specialized training in psychiatry and some forms of psychotherapy, typically including up to five hundred hours of direct clinical experience. Psychiatric nurses in most states may also carry prescription privileges, meaning that they can often prescribe the same kinds of medications that a psychiatrist can.

Psychiatrist
A psychiatrist is a medical doctor and the only professional who specializes in mental health care *and* can prescribe medications. (Family doctors often prescribe medications for mental health concerns, but do not have specialized training or background in treating mental disorders.) Most psychiatrists focus on prescribing the appropriate medication that's going to work best for that individual and their concerns; a few also do psychotherapy.

Psychologist (PhD or PsyD)
A psychologist is a professional who does psychotherapy and has a doctorate degree (such as a PhD or PsyD). PsyD programs tend to focus on clinical practice and result in the professional having thousands of hours of clinical experience before they enter practice. PhD programs can focus on either clinical or research work, and the amount of clinical experience a professional will gain varies from program to program. Psychologists receive specific training in diagnosis, psychological assessment, a wide variety of psychotherapies, research, and more.

Registered Nurse (RN)
To become a registered nurse, an individual can complete a diploma program offered by a hospital nursing school, receive an associate degree in nursing (ADN) at a community college, or a bachelor's degree in nursing (BSN) at a college or university. Graduates of any of the programs must pass a state licensing exam before they are qualified for staff positions as a registered nurse.

PSYCHIATRIC TERMS

Affective disorder: A mental disorder in which the main symptom is an abnormal mood; usually depression or mania.

Affect: The emotional tone a person expresses. A person's affect may be appropriate or inappropriate. One type of inappropriate affect is blunted or flat; another is labile, which means emotions are varied, sometimes enraged.

Alogia: A poverty of words, or a reduction in the amount of speech. This is often found in schizophrenia.

Agoraphobia: A disorder which involves intense fear and anxiety of any place or situation where escape might be difficult, leading to avoidance of situations such as being alone outside of the home; traveling in a car, bus, or airplane; or being in a crowded area. People who suffer from this disorder are unwilling and afraid to leave their house and interact with the public. It can be a result of panic disorder (the reason they do not leave is because they are afraid they will have a panic attack in public).

Akathisia (restless leg syndrome): A person may have extreme jitters or restlessness, such as rocking from foot to foot, walking in place, pacing, or an inability to sit still. It can be a side effect of certain classes of medications (neuroleptics or atypical antipsychotics), but there are other causes. It is not the same as psychomotor agitation, which sometimes accompanies mental illness.

Anhedonia: An inability to enjoy activities that normally give pleasure. It is described by some as "deadness" in the brain.

Anosognosia: A lack of insight or deficit of self-awareness; the condition in which a person who suffers from a mental illness seems unaware of its existence because their brain, which gives insight, is damaged.

Anticholinergic: An anticholinergic agent is a substance that blocks the neurotransmitter acetylcholine, a substance produced by the body that causes certain nervous system activities. Drugs with anticholinergic effects include antidepressants, antihistamines, and antipsychotics.

Antidepressants: Medication used to treat depression by regulating neurotransmitters of the brain, such as serotonin, norepinephrine and dopamine (see Appendix C: Overview of Medications).

Antipsychotic (neuroleptic): Medication used to treat psychosis. They were once informally called major tranquilizers, because of their sedative effects. The newer class of "atypical" antipsychotic has some antidepressant effect and some effect on the recurrence of major depression and bipolar disorder. Atypical drugs have fewer side effects than the older antipsychotics.

Anxiety: A vague state of emotional distress, associated with feelings of nervous tension, uncertainty, and fear. Physical responses include palpitations of the heart, increased blood pressure, fainting, shortness of breath, and rapid breathing. Neuromuscular responses include twitching of eyelids, tremors, and startle reaction. Gastrointestinal responses include diarrhea, heartburn, and abdominal discomfort. The person can feel and look flushed and generally sweating.

Anxiety disorder: A number of disorders are placed in the category of anxiety disorders. Among them are generalized anxiety, phobias, post-traumatic stress disorder, panic disorder, obsessive compulsive disorder, agoraphobia, socialized anxiety disorder, and somatoform disorder. No two people with anxiety have the same experiences, but all anxiety disorders have one thing in common: persistent, excessive fear or worry in situations that are not threatening. Anxiety disorders respond to antidepressants, especially SSRIs (selective serotonin reuptake inhibitors)

Attention Deficit Hyperactivity Disorder (ADHD): One of the most common childhood disorders, which can continue through adolescence and adulthood. Symptoms include difficulty staying focused and paying attention, difficulty controlling behavior, and hyperactivity (overactivity). ADHD has three subtypes: predominantly hyperactive-impulsive; predominantly inattentive; combined hyperactive-impulsive and inattentive.

Autism Spectrum Disorder (ASD): The name for a group of developmental disorders. ASD includes a wide range (spectrum) of symptoms, skills, and levels of disability. Repetitive behaviors may include moving objects or parts of objects; repeating certain behaviors, or having unusual behaviors; having overly focused interests; or ongoing social problems that include difficulty communicating and interacting with others.

Avolitional: A severe lack of initiative or motivation; the willpower of a person fails to achieve certain goals and outcomes that have to do with everyday living skills. This can sometimes interfere with relationships, since others complain that he or she just doesn't care. Avolition is found in schizophrenia.

Bipolar disorder (manic-depressive disorder): An affective disorder that causes severe and unusually high and low shifts in mood, energy, and activity levels. A manic episode can begin with a pleasurable sense of heightened energy, poor decision-making, creativity, social ease, bursts of anger, and racing thoughts. The low end of the disorder is classic depression with psychomotor retardation and feelings of sadness and hopelessness.

Blunting of affect: A lack of emotion; the voice may become monotone and one's facial expression may not change.

Catatonia: The catatonic state involves movements and behaviors that are inappropriately excessive, repetitive, purposeless, or unresponsive. The body becomes rigid or the person goes into a stupor or unresponsiveness to his or her environment. This is associated with a breakdown of neurotransmitters in the brain and a disturbed mental state.

Central nervous system (CNS): The brain and spinal cord. The CNS is responsible for coordinating the activities of all parts of the brain and spinal cord.

Cognition: Conscious mental activities (such as thinking, communicating, understanding, problem-solving, processing information, and remembering) that are associated with gaining knowledge and understanding.

Cognitive behavioral therapy (CBT): CBT helps people focus on how to solve their current problems. The therapist helps the patient learn how to identify distorted or unhelpful thinking patterns, recognize and change inaccurate beliefs, relate to others in more positive ways, and change behaviors accordingly.

Comorbidity: The existence of two or more illnesses in the same person. These illnesses can be physical or mental.

Delusion: A fixed false belief that makes incorrect inferences about external reality. This belief is steadfastly maintained in spite of contrary evidence. Delusions of grandeur involve incorrect perceptions of the self (inflating personal power or knowledge, or relationship to deity).

Dementia: An organic deterioration of mental faculties including the ability to reason and memory; characterized by confusion and disorientation. This can be the result of stroke, aging, or Alzheimer's disease.

Depersonalization: A feeling associated with anxiety disorders, that one is becoming unreal or is separated from his/her own body or thoughts. Sometimes it is likened to a dream state or looking at one's actions in kaleidoscope fashion.

Derealization: A dreamlike feeling associated with anxiety disorders that the observable world and its experiences are strange or not real—for example, the world seems to be slowing down, or reality is viewed as in a fog or from the inside of a fishbowl.

Disorientation: Confusion within a person concerning self-identity or surroundings. It may become difficult to relate to the current day and time.

Dissociative state: Detachment from one's own identity and memories, usually occurring when reality seems too frightening. Sexual abuse victims sometimes experience this kind of withdrawal. The term is used to describe what happens in a person who seems to have multiple personalities. There is disagreement among psychiatrists and psychologists about whether true dissociative states occur and what forms they take.

Dopamine: A neurotransmitter found in high concentrations in the limbic system in the brain. It is involved in the regulation of movement, thought and behavior, and pleasurable rewarding sensations.

Dual diagnosis: Having a mental health disorder and an alcohol or drug problem at the same time.

Dystonia: Movement disorders in which sustained muscle contractions cause involuntary and sometimes painful twisting and repetitive movements or abnormal postures. Birth injury (particularly due to lack of oxygen), certain infections, heavy-metal or carbon monoxide poisoning, trauma, or stroke can cause dystonic symptoms. It can be caused by taking certain forms of antipsychotic medicine. The main features are sticking out the tongue, abnormal head position, grimacing, neck spasms, and eyes rolling up.

Early intervention: Diagnosing and treating a mental illness when it first develops.

Electroconvulsive therapy (ECT): Formerly called electroshock therapy; used to treat serious depression, catatonic schizophrenia, and mania. It is considered to be the most effective treatment of severe depression. ECT includes a controlled convulsion caused by the passing of an electrical current through a targeted portion of the brain. The person is given a mild anesthetic and the drug Succinylcholine, which minimizes the convulsive effects in the body but not the brain.

Exposure therapy: A technique in behavior therapy used to treat anxiety disorders. It involves the exposure of the patient to the feared object or context without any danger, in order to overcome their anxiety and/or distress.

Extrapyramidal symptom (EPS): A disturbance of facial or body movements, such as muscle stiffness, tremors, and lack of arm movement when walking. It can be a side effect of antipsychotic (neuroleptic) medication. The dystonias are EPS difficulties. See also **dystonia**.

Flashback: A recurrence of a memory, feeling, or perceptual experience from the past. It is common for those with post-traumatic stress disorder, or who have suffered sexual or extreme physical abuse, to have flashbacks that relive the experiences.

Flight of ideas: A rapid flow of ideas in the brain that produces pressured (accelerated) speech, with quick changes in topic and subject matters, sometimes based on association of thoughts or a "play on words." This can also be known as loose association.

Functional Magnetic Resonance Imaging (fMRI, or functional MRI): A functional neuroimaging procedure using MRI technology that measures brain activity by detecting changes associated with blood flow. This technique relies on the fact that cerebral blood flow and neuronal activation are coupled.

Hallucination: A false perception of reality, with sounds, sights, smells, or tastes that are not coming from the real world. They are categorized by the type of sensory experience involved: Hallucinations can be visual, auditory, tactile, gustatory, and/or olfactory

Hypersomnia: Excessive sleepiness evidenced by a "deep" sleep, which sometimes lasts from ten to sixteen hours.

Inappropriate affect: Emotional or behavioral actions that do not fit the situation, such as laughing when hearing bad news.

Insomnia: A disturbance in sleep patterns in which the individual cannot fall asleep (initial insomnia), wakes frequently (middle insomnia), or wakes after insufficient sleep and does not return to sleep (terminal insomnia). Chronic insomnia is associated with any of a number of causes for the "circadian rhythms" of the brain to work improperly.

Intervention: An action intended to help treat or cure a condition.

Limbic system: A group of brain structures, composed of the hippocampus and amygdala, associated with memory storage, coordination of autonomic functions, and the control of mood and emotion.

Long-acting injectable (drugs): A shot of medication administered once or twice a month. The shot is an alternative to taking a daily dose of medication.

Usually effective when given to a person with no insight into their illness, especially schizophrenia, since they can be confused and not be able to remember or know how to take their medications as needed.

Luteal phase: The post-ovulatory portion of a woman's cycle (i.e., the time between when a woman ovulates and when she gets her period).

Magnetic resonance imaging (MRI): Diagnostic technique using magnetism, radio waves, and a computer to produce images of body structures. The image and resolution produced is detailed enough to detect tiny changes of structures. The scanner is a tube surrounded by a giant circular magnet. The patient is passed through the magnetic field, which aligns the protons of hydrogen atoms, which are then exposed to a beam of radio waves. The image produced is detected by a receiver and processed by computer.

Major depressive disorder: An affective disorder characterized by severe and long-lasting bouts of depression. Symptoms can include a lack of appetite or increased appetite, poor concentration, feelings of hopelessness, severe sleep disturbance, and profound feelings of sadness and worthlessness. Suicidal thoughts and psychomotor agitation or retardation are usually present at some points.

Mania: A state of mind and mood characterized by euphoria or irritability, rapid speech, insomnia, distractibility, grandiosity, and poor judgment. The person may have delusions, auditory or visual hallucinations, and a "racing mind."

Manic depression: See also **bipolar disorder.**

Mental illness: Any serious disorder affecting thought, mood, or behavior. The disorders can be on a continuum of mild, moderate, and severe. The mood symptoms are often episodic. Schizophrenia is regarded as the most debilitating type of mental illness.

Mood: Sustained emotional state that colors perception. Moods can be characterized by states of depression, elation, anger, and anxiety. In contrast to affect, which refers to more fluctuating changes in emotion, mood refers to more pervasive and sustained emotional climate.

Mood disorder: Mental disorders primarily affecting a person's mood.

Negative symptoms: Symptoms of schizophrenia are often classified as positive or negative. Examples of negative symptoms that "take away" from life include social withdrawal, lost interest in life, low energy, emotional flatness, alogia, and avolitional reduced ability to concentrate and remember. See also **positive symptoms.**

Neurotransmitter: Molecules that carry chemical messages between nerve cells. These messages either excite or inhibit a synaptic signal. Neurotransmitters are released from neurons, diffuse across the minute space between cells (synaptic cleft), and bind to receptors located on postsynaptic neuronal surfaces. The neurotransmitters are acetylcholine, dopamine, epinephrine, norepinephrine, serotonin, glutamate, glycine, and gaminobutric acid (GABA).

Panic attack: Intense anxiety states of panic, fear, or dread that can come upon a person instantly, with or without a trigger from surroundings. Some panic attacks attach to phobias. The attack is accompanied by such symptoms as shortness of breath, racing heartbeat, and a fear of dying or "going crazy."

Paranoid ideation: Ideas that are formulated and become fixed in the mind. They may or may not have any basis in fact and they are not as serious as delusions, which are altogether false. These ideas usually relate to general suspicion or a belief that one is being singled out to be harassed, persecuted, or treated unfairly.

Paranoid-type schizophrenia: Profound mental illness characterized by life-controlling delusions. There are usually auditory hallucinations and may be accompanied by incoherent or illogical speech, disorganized behavior, and/or inappropriate emotions and behaviors.

Parasuicidal behavior: Intentional self-injury resulting in actual tissue damage, illness, or risk of death. It is frequently the type of behavior shown in the taking of overdoses of medicines, probably without a strong final resolution to commit suicide.

Personality disorder: Personality disorders are psychological conditions that appear in adolescence or early adulthood, continue over many years, and cause a great deal of distress. Personality disorders often disrupt a person's ability to enjoy life or find fulfillment in relationships, work, or school. Unlike the major mental illnesses, the main treatment of personality disorder is not through medication. People with personality disorders have multiple problems, characteristics, and concerns. They also can suffer a mental illness (comorbidity). For instance, many women with borderline personal disorder often have major depression and post-traumatic stress syndrome.

Phobia: Irrational fear of a situation or object. Any contact or association with the thing feared or thoughts of it can cause a panic attack. The person with the phobia will try to avoid the feared situation or trigger. Some develop *agoraphobia*. To avoid triggers, the agoraphobic person will come to fear and avoid any new environment at all. Agoraphobia sufferers often become prisoners in their homes. See also **panic attack**.

Positive symptoms: Symptoms of schizophrenia are often classified as positive or negative. Examples of positive symptoms that "add to" a person's experiences include delusions (believing something to be true when it is not) and hallucinations (seeing, hearing, feeling, smelling or tasting something that is not real). See also **negative symptoms**

Positron emission tomography (PET scan): Diagnostic tool in which a radioactive substance is injected, travels to the brain, and shows up as relative bright structures on an image. Pet scans have helped in the study of brain changes relating to mental illness.

Psychomotor agitation: Excessive motor activity associated with a feeling of inner tension. It manifests itself in such behaviors as wringing hands, pulling hair, and constant pacing or rocking. It is often part of a mood disorder.

Psychomotor retardation: Generalized slowing of the physical, mental, and emotional reactions. It is often seen in depression, especially the depressive phase of manic depression.

Psychosis: Generally defined as an abnormal perception of reality or cognitive function. It distorts reality and often is accompanied by delusions and/or hallucinations. The person experiencing a psychotic episode usually cannot distinguish reality from fantasy.

Psychosocial Intervention: Non-medication therapies for people with mental illness and their families. Therapies include psychotherapy, coping skills, training, and supported employment and education services.

Psychotherapy: Literally "healing of the mind"; a concept with strong historical ties to Freudian views of treatment by probing the subconscious for keys to problems that affect the conscious. Most common psychotherapies today use cognitive-behavioral, interpersonal, and reflective listening techniques. Most psychotherapists today are not psychiatrists but licensed professionals in fields of psychology, counseling, and/or social work.

Psychotropic: Any chemical formulation used in treatment of mental illness that affects brain and neurological functioning, behavior, or experience. Psychotropics include antipsychotic, antidepressant, anti-mania, stimulant, and antianxiety medications.

Recovery: The process by which people with mental illness return or begin to work, learn and participate in their communities. For some individuals and their families, recovery means the ability to live a fulfilling and productive life.

Schizoaffective disorder: A condition that includes chronic symptoms of schizophrenia and also episodes of affective disorder (either bipolar or depressive).

Schizophrenia: A chronic, disabling brain disease with symptoms including delusions, hallucinations, disorganized thoughts, or grossly disorganized or catatonic behavior. Other symptoms include a lack of emotion, an inability to react to surroundings, or trouble communicating. Symptoms may leave them fearful and withdrawn. Their speech and behavior can be so disorganized that they may be incomprehensible or frightening to others. No more than one in five recovers completely.

Serotonin: Neurotransmitter that relays impulses between nerve cells (neurons) in the central nervous system. Functions thought to be regulated by nerve cells that use serotonin include mood and behavior, physical coordination, appetite, body temperature, and sleep.

Serotonin-dopamine antagonist (SDA): "Atypical" antipsychotic medicine, which treats positive and negative symptoms of schizophrenia and other serious mental illnesses with fewer side effects. Examples include Seroquel (quetiapine fumarate), Clozaril (clozapine), Zyprexa (olanzapine), Risperdal (risperidone), and Geodon (ziprasidone).

Typical antipsychotics: Also called conventional antipsychotics or neuroleptics; medications first developed in the 1950s to treat psychosis and especially schizophrenia. Typical antipsychotics may also be used for the treatment of acute mania, agitation, and other conditions. They are being replaced by atypical antipsychotics, which are more effective generally and have fewer side effects, such as EPS, in patients.

SPIRITUAL TERMS

Darkness (spiritual): People who are clinically depressed are often in spiritual darkness. I remember after I had been moderately depressed for a long time, I was asked by my friend to call his sister and talk with her about depression. I shared with her that I felt like was in a big dark room and that Jesus was next to me in the room, though I could not see or feel him. She replied, "I feel like I am in a big dark room and Jesus is not in the room; he is outside. That is the difference between a Christian being in the dark and an unbeliever being there."

Demon: Demons are active in today's world. The word *daimon* or *daimonion* seems to involve a general reference, leads to the application of the term to the peculiar and restricted class of beings designated "demons" in the New Testament.

Demon possession: The actual possession of a man or woman by a demon, taking control of their soul and spirit. Demons cannot possess a Christian (1 John 5:18); however, they can harass (oppress) believers, which results in harm to the one harassed or to someone else. Such was the case of Peter and the Lord (Matt. 16:21–24). Peter had a flawed eschatology (doctrine of things to come), as did the other eleven disciples. Peter fell into the devil's deception when he actually rebuked the Lord for saying that His one great mission was to die on the cross.

We know that no one who is born of God sins; but that He who was born of God keeps him, and the evil one does not touch him.

Demoralization: Demoralization is caused by a specific stress or stressors which undermine the confidence or the morale of a person. It means "to deprive (a person or persons) of spirit, courage, discipline, to destroy the morale of someone or some group of people."

Depression (spiritual): Probably the greatest work in the last two centuries on this topic is the book by D. Martyn Lloyd-Jones called *Spiritual Depression: Its Causes and Cures.*

There were people in the Bible who experienced spiritual depression. This depression is not a biological problem; it is the result of the spirit of man feeling forsaken, angry, or disappointed. The Bible characters are like we are; they expressed the emotions they felt and sometimes they failed, and, at times, they definitely misunderstood God and his purposes. Spiritual depression is tied to a lack of understanding God's love for His child. It has to do with the spirit of a person who is a believer in Christ. The Bible also calls it a broken spirit. The causes are numerous:

> **"We were cheated":** The people in Nehemiah 8 felt cheated because their temple was not as magnificent as Solomon's temple. Many of the old men, who had seen the first temple, wept loudly when the foundation of the house was laid before their eyes. It seemed so small to them. They were told that the joy of the Lord would be their strength.

> **Disappointment with God:** Elijah was disappointed. He misunderstood the purpose of the Baal encounter and asked God to kill him after an amazing miraculous feat on Mt. Carmel. He became woefully depressed. We see him in the desert, and at Sinai. The LORD was so very compassionate toward him. Here was a man who wanted to die—and yet, he is one of two men in the Bible who never died at all. Elijah was taken to heaven in a cloud, never to be disappointed again and understanding God's entire plan for his life.

> **Discontentment:** Asaph lost his contentment by envying the prosperous wicked. God restored Him and in the last part of Psalm 73, he shares the delight of seeing a loving God who would be His portion, now and in Heaven.

> **Chastening:** It could be the result of discipline, which a true child of God must endure. David, for example, describes his one year of depression in Psalm 32 and the effects it had on his physical body.

> **"What's the use?":** Job, grieving the loss of his children and all his possessions, moaned that the worst part of all was losing God's presence. Spiritual depression could also come from having a lack of assurance of salvation, or from giving into fleshly lusts, which wage war against the soul.

> **John the Baptist:** John was the forerunner of Christ. As he sat in a damp, dark dungeon, he wondered whether Jesus was really the One they thought He was. He was spiritually depressed.

Spiritual depression can affect anyone; anyone who knows Christ is subject to the temptation to doubt, fall, question the Lord, and want to give up. We must fight while we have the opportunity; learn from these great people of faith who temporarily lost sight of the God Who called them to serve, and trust and fight the temptation to fall into a lonely, sad, and depressing spiritual state.

Desertion, apparent: The doctrine of God's apparent desertion in the Bible is where a child of God cannot feel the sensible presence of the Lord, known in Scripture as "the face of the Lord" or the shining face of the Lord, as seen in Isaiah 50:10:

> Who is among you that fears the LORD, That obeys the voice of His servant, That walks in darkness and has no light? Let him trust in the name of the LORD and rely on his God.

This passage is speaking of a believer, since the prophet puts him in the category of "those among you who fears the Lord."[40] The word LORD is that of Yahweh the special name for the covenant keeping "God of Israel." The darkness does not mean a sinful judgment or even chastisement but he who cannot feel or sense the affirming love of God in all his worship and service. It is like the case of the Psalmist when he said,

> Now as for me, I said in my prosperity, "I will never be moved." O LORD, by Your favor You have made my mountain to stand strong; You hid Your face, I was dismayed (Ps. 30:6–7).

It must be said that many a Christian has been in the dark by chastisement or heavy trial. But, this is not because God has deserted him. The only man that was ever deserted by God was the Son of God. He expressed His deep sorrow as he became sin for us that we might have His righteousness. In the true desertion that Christ experienced, He cried out, "My God, My God, why have you forsaken me?" We may *feel* alone but we are never truly alone, nor forsaken, when we know Christ as Savior.

> For I am convinced that neither death, nor life, nor angels, nor principalities, nor things present, nor things to come, nor powers, nor height, nor depth, nor any other created thing, will be able to separate us from the love of God, which is in Christ Jesus our Lord (Rom. 8:38–39).

> Then Job answered, "Oh, that my grief was actually weighed. And lay in the balances together with my calamity! For then it would be heavier than the sand of the seas; therefore my words have been rash. For the arrows of the Almighty are within me, their poison my spirit drinks; the terrors of God are arrayed against me" (Job 6:1–4).

Job, who stands as our profound example in trials, lost all of his children and everything he possessed, and then he also laments losing God's sensible presence, saying,

> Oh, that I were as in months gone by, as in the days when God watched over me; when His lamp shone over my head, and by His light I walked through

darkness; as I was in the prime of my days, when the friendship of God was over my tent; when the Almighty was yet with me, and my children were around me; when my steps were bathed in butter, and the rock poured out for me streams of oil! (Job 29:2–6).

Furthermore, his friends who sat with him were unfeeling, foolish, cruel, exacting, critical, and deceptive—all parts of another element which that fiend, Satan, was permitted to bring to the equation. When at first they saw him from afar, they wept, seeing their friend in such a condition. Then, in those early days, they sat and said nothing. As the days wore on and nothing about Job's condition improved, they began to reason; there had to be an explanation as to why Job was in such agony of mind, body, and spirit. He must have done something wrong and it must have been far worse than they would have ever expected. This is the point where they spoke in cruel and upsetting words to a man trying to make sense of a life turned upside down. They were obviously being directed by the devil, which not only controlled them, but tempted them with appalling pride.

When a man of God cannot find his Father in a trial, there is nothing worse. Job could not find the face of God. He doubted His lovingkindness. He lost His presence. He could not understand why he had to endure such suffering in extremis.

Do you know, pastor, that there are people in your flock who feel this way?

One group of those who feel deserted and alone is the mentally ill. They do not feel they can appropriately share their grief or sadness or pain. The average person does not understand it and they have read all the self-help books, prayed the Psalms, listened to radio pastors and counselors, and like the woman with the issue of blood for eighteen years, they have spent all their money and nothing has changed. They have also worn out their supporters and they cannot find the Lord they love.

The apostle Paul felt this and wrote about his apparent desertion by God in 2 Corinthians:

> For we do not want you to be unaware, brethren, of our affliction which came to us in Asia, that we were burdened excessively, beyond our strength, so that we despaired even of life; indeed, we had the sentence of death within ourselves so that we would not trust in ourselves, but in God who raises the dead; who delivered us from so great a peril of death, and will deliver us He on whom we have set our hope. And He will yet deliver us, you also joining in helping us through your prayers, so that thanks may be given by many persons on our behalf for the favor bestowed on us through the prayers of many (2 Cor. 1:8–11).

The brains of believers are dying; some have schizophrenia, some have bipolar disorder, some have been dealt the disease of Alzheimer's, and some have experienced a stroke. When the brain is sick, the thinking and the mood will be affected. These sick sheep need encouragement and consolation. Paul further said, "The body is dead because of sin, but the spirit is alive because of righteousness" (Rom. 8:10).

The Bible is a body of inspired books, and within those books are stories of people like us interacting with God and with others. The Lord has given us not just facts, but insight into what made them who they were. We can read about their successes and failures and watch them react to God—either as Judge or Savior. When they made mistakes, we see them; when they struggle, we see that, too. What we have is an honest perspective of these players on the biblical stage. We are not shown only heroes but heroes who faltered and feared; some cowards, some encouragers, some warriors and some who didn't feel very valiant.

Gideon is such a man. He has his own place in history and we are privileged to know how he felt when the apparent desertion of God was in his soul. By temperament, his own description of his pedigree and his training, Gideon was a man who was weak. We find him alone, threshing wheat at night; why? Because he feared the Midianites were going to kill him. The Scripture says, the angel of the LORD appeared to him and said to him, "The LORD is with you, valiant warrior" (Judg. 6:12).

Gideon saw the preincarnate Christ—and like many other Bible characters, he did not recognize Him. Gideon was sitting next to Him and was talking with Him. The LORD of Hosts was going to give Gideon an effective battle plan but Gideon insists that the LORD had abandoned His people, Israel. Then Gideon said to him:

> O my lord, if the LORD is with us, why then has all this happened to us? And where are all His miracles which our fathers told us about, saying, "did not the LORD bring us up from Egypt?" But now the LORD has abandoned us and given us into, the hand of Midian (Judg. 6:13).

The irony here is that Gideon, depressed and doubtful of any power to defeat the Midianites, actually received a commission and promise of empowerment from the Lord Himself to save Israel—and then Gideon carps and complains of the LORD's lack of support for Israel.

> The LORD looked at him and said, "Go in this your strength and deliver Israel from the hand of Midian. Have I not sent you?" (Judg. 6:14).

His depression showed that he did not believe the covenantal promises found in the law, which stated that if they were obedient to the word of God, God would defeat their enemies. But God did not give up on Gideon. God desires to do great things through weak people.

The Westminster Shorter Catechism says:

> True believers may have the assurance of their salvation divers ways shaken, diminished, and intermitted; as, by negligence in preserving of it, by falling

into some special sin which wounds the conscience and grieves the Spirit; by some sudden or vehement temptation, by God's withdrawing the light of His countenance, and suffering even such as fear Him to walk in darkness and to have no light yet are they never so utterly destitute of that seed of God, and life of faith, that love of Christ and the brethren, that sincerity of heart, and conscience of duty, out of which, by the operation of the Spirit, this assurance may, in due time, be revived and by the which, in the mean-time, they are supported from utter despair.[41]

An important thing about those who feel that they are deserted is that they do not have a biblical understanding of what is called, "The face of the Lord." The face of the Lord is the sensible joy of His presence. "Why do You hide Your face, and forget our affliction and our oppression? For our soul has sunk down into the dust; our body cleaves to the earth. Rise up, be our help, and redeem us for the sake of Your lovingkindness" (Ps. 44:24–26).

RESEARCH AND TREATMENT

What's different between the brains of healthy people and those with depression? A major breakthrough study regarding depression, using fMRI brain scans from more than a thousand participants, was done in order to answer that question.[42] What it found is that within the umbrella category of "people who have major depressive disorder," there exist (at least) four distinct neurotypes, each with its own cluster of associated symptoms. And the neurotypes aren't random. They align with their symptom clusters along two major axes: anxiety and anhedonia (the inability to feel pleasure). The authors refer to the axes as a shared pathological core, by which we can understand the relationship between brain connectivity and the symptoms of depression. These newly discovered patterns of abnormal connectivity are biomarkers for depression—something neuroscience had been chasing for a long while without much success.

We've now finally nailed down that depression is really a full-blown systemic neurodegenerative disease, rather than a simple chemical imbalance—and that these pathologic changes in brain progress if the depression is not effectively treated. Another new thing we've learned is that almost all antidepressants significantly improve neuroplasticity and neurogenesis. We are beginning to finally understand the origins and symptoms of depression.

SCHIZOPHRENIA

"Schizophrenia, which occurs in around 1% of the U.S. adult population, is a "chronic, severe and disabling mental disorder characterized by deficits in thought processes, perceptions and emotional responsiveness," according to the National Institute of Mental Health.[43] People with schizophrenia can experience a variety of debilitating symptoms, including visual and aural hallucinations and an aversion to social interactions.

Experts have long struggled to pinpoint the disorder's biological roots — until now. After a widespread genetic analysis of 65,000 people, researchers from the Broad Institute's Stanley Center for Psychiatric Research, Harvard Medical School, Boston Children's Hospital, and Massachusetts General Hospital found an increased risk of schizophrenia among people with a particular variant of a gene called "complement component 4," or C4.

C4 plays a role in a biological process called "synaptic pruning"— the severance of connections between neurons. That makes sense, a press release stated. Not only is synaptic pruning more prevalent during adolescence—the age when schizophrenia symptoms typically appear—but people with schizophrenia have been found to have fewer connections between neurons in their brains than people who don't have schizophrenia.

Hope for the future: According to a statement from Bruce Cuthbert, acting director of the National Institute of Mental Health, this discovery "changes the game" when it comes to fighting mental illness.

"Thanks to this genetic breakthrough, we can finally see the potential for clinical tests, early detection, new treatments, and even prevention," he said.

For Nicole Amesbury, a licensed mental health counselor, people with schizophrenia still encounter intense societal stigma. "When someone gets diagnosed with cancer, there are 5k races and people rallying around them," Amesbury said. "If someone gets diagnosed with schizophrenia, oftentimes those people are treated like pariahs."[44]

DEPRESSION

Clinical depression is more than just the "blues," being "down in the dumps," or experiencing temporary feelings of sadness we all have from time to time in our lives. It is a serious condition that affects a person's mind and body. It impacts all aspects of everyday life including eating, sleeping, working, relationships, and how a person thinks about himself/herself. People who are clinically depressed cannot simply will themselves to feel better or just "snap out of it." If they do not receive appropriate treatment their symptoms can continue for weeks, months, or years.

The good news is that very effective treatments are available to help those who are depressed. However, only about one-third of those who are depressed actually receive treatment. This is unfortunate since upwards of 80-90% of those who do seek treatment can feel better within just a few weeks. Many people do not seek treatment for depression for a variety of reasons. Some believe that depression is the result of a personal weakness or character flaw. This is simply not true. Like diabetes, heart disease, or any other medical condition, clinical depression is an illness that should be treated by a mental health professional or physician. Another reason why many people do not seek help for depression is that they simply do not recognize the signs or symptoms that something may be wrong.

Depression affects approximately 19 million Americans, or 9.5% of the population in any given one-year period. At some point in their lives, 10%–25% of women and 5%–12% of men will likely become clinically depressed. It affects so many people that it is often referred to as the "common cold" of mental illness. It is estimated that depression exacts an economic cost of over $30 billion each year, but the cost of human suffering cannot be measured. Depression not only causes suffering to those who are depressed, but it also causes great difficulty for their family and friends who often do not know how to help.

Additional Statistics and Information about Depression

- Major depression is the leading cause of disability in the United States.
- Depression affects roughly 19 million Americans in a given year.
- During their lifetime, 10%–25% of women and 5%–12% of men will become clinically depressed.
- Women are affected by depression almost twice as often as men.
- The economic cost of depression is estimated to be more than $30 billion each year.
- Two-thirds of those who are depressed never seek treatment and suffer needlessly.
- Eighty to ninety percent of those who seek treatment for depression can feel better within just a few weeks.
- Research on twins suggests that there is a genetic component to the risk of developing depression.
- Research has also shown that the stress of a loss, especially the death of a loved one, may lead to depression in some people.

MENTAL HEALTH DISORDERS IN CHILDREN

It is important that pastors be aware that mental illness affects many children. The prevalence of mental health disorders among young people in this country approximates that of adults, and their impact may be even greater in youth because they strike during critical periods of educational, emotional, and social development. It is estimated that 17.1 million young people have or have had a diagnosable psychiatric disorder.[45]

Put another way, twenty percent of US children—one in five—have a mental health disorder. Fifty percent of mental health disorders begin before age fourteen, and seventy-five percent before age twenty-four, affecting the learning and school experience for all children.

These are disorders of childhood and adolescence that, if untreated, will have a marked effect on students' ability to learn and function in the school environment. For instance:

- Seventy-five percent of social phobias manifest by age fifteen.
- Seventy-five percent of separation anxiety disorders manifest by age ten.
- Seventy-five percent of oppositional defiant disorders manifest by age fourteen.
- Seventy-five percent of ADHD cases manifest by age eight.

Anxiety disorders like social phobia can make students twice as likely to drop out or fail a grade;[46] ADHD, mood and anxiety symptoms, and disruptive behavior at age six predict math and reading achievement at age seventeen; and combinations of mental health disorders (including substance abuse) are predictors for low levels of lifetime educational attainment.[47]

TREATMENTS FOR MENTAL ILLNESS

Electroconvulsive Therapy

Electroconvulsive therapy (ECT) was originally developed as a treatment for those with schizophrenia in 1938. By the 1980s it had become useful for those suffering with severe depression, treatment-resistant depression (depression that has not abated by treatment with at least two antidepressants), psychotic depression, and patients who are suicidal. More than half of all those who receive ECT respond favorably within the first four weeks.

Patients are anesthetized and either one or two electrodes are placed on the patient's skull to induce seizures. If the electrodes are placed on only one side of the brain, there seems to be less memory loss and other cognitive impairments. Patients who receive ECT show response rates of seventy to ninety percent over a span of differing degrees of depression, but those with treatment-resistant depression showed less success. Active maintenance ECT, or a medication regime, is recommended to prevent further episodes.

Trans-cranial Magnetic Stimulation

Trans-cranial magnetic stimulation (TMS) is a brain stimulation technique using electromagnetic induction and a rapidly changing magnetic field to induce weak electric currents, which cause depolarization or hyperpolarization of neurons in specific parts of the brain."[48]

TMS is a noninvasive procedure that uses magnetic fields to stimulate nerve cells in the brain to improve symptoms of depression, and is typically used when other depression treatments haven't been effective. Treatment for depression involves delivering repetitive magnetic pulses, so it's called repetitive TMS or rTMS.[49]

During a TMS session, an electromagnetic coil is placed against your scalp near your forehead. The electromagnet painlessly delivers a magnetic pulse that stimulates nerve cells in the region of your brain involved in mood control and depression. It may also activate regions of the brain that have decreased activity in people with depression.

Though the biology of why TMS works isn't completely understood, the stimulation appears to affect how this part of the brain is working, which in turn seems to ease depression symptoms and improve mood.

Vagus Nerve Stimulation

"Vagus nerve stimulation includes a surgical implant that stimulates electrically the ascending branch of the left vagus nerve and stimulates the vagal nucleus of the solitary tract…VNS has been used as an anticonvulsant and was adapted as an antidepressant treatment after positive effects on mood were noticed in patients receiving the treatment for epilepsy."[50]

Vagus nerve stimulation (VNS) has been used for chronic depression and treatment-resistant depression. Since most insurance companies do not cover this treatment and it is a surgical procedure, the implantations have not been used very often. The side effects include neck or jaw pain, neck pain, cough, or hoarseness after procedure.

Deep Brain Stimulation

"Deep Brain Stimulation (DBS) is a surgical procedure used to treat a variety of disabling neurological symptoms—most commonly the debilitating symptoms of Parkinson's disease (PD), such as tremor, rigidity, stiffness, slowed movement, and walking problems."[51] It is also "an investigational treatment for depression involving direct stimulation of specific subcortical brain areas to affect the brain neurocircuitry of emotional regulation."[52]

Ketamine

Ketamine is an anesthetic that has been around for decades. Intravenous ketamine was the anesthetic of choice for outpatient procedures in children when I was in medical training nearly forty years ago. Twenty years ago, ketamine achieved notoriety as a recreational drug under the moniker "Special K." But in the past decade, ketamine has emerged as a potential antidepressant.

Recent data suggest that ketamine, given intravenously, might be the most important breakthrough in antidepressant treatment in decades. First and most important, several studies demonstrate that ketamine reduces depression within six hours, with effects that are equal to or greater than the effects of six weeks of treatment with other antidepressant medications.[53]

Second, ketamine's effects have been noted in people with treatment-resistant depression. This promises a new option for people with some of the most disabling and chronic forms of depression, whether classified as major depressive disorder or bipolar depression.

Third, it appears that one of the earliest effects of the drug is a profound reduction in suicidal thoughts. We have not had medications that were specifically antisuicidal, and though it may be too early to label ketamine as an antisuicide medication, there has been a reduction in people with severe, treatment-resistant depression. But there is enough potential here that several universities and companies have launched research and development efforts.

It is also used for obsessive-compulsive disorder and post-traumatic stress disorder.[54] Recently the Food and Drug Administration awarded breakthrough therapy designation for the development of intranasal ketamine for treating depression. This is the first time that this special designation—usually reserved for drugs targeting an epidemic or a deadly form of cancer—has been awarded for the development of a mental disorder medication. This speaks to the scientific opportunity and the public health need for having a rapid antidepressant.

That need is leading to ketamine clinics using this drug "off-label" to treat depression. While the science is promising, ketamine is not ready for broad use in the clinic. We just don't know enough about either efficacy or safety. But with the excitement generated by early results, we will have more information soon. The doom and gloom surrounding medication development, at least for depression, seems to be rapidly resolving.[55]

THE MAJOR MENTAL ILLNESSES

Mental illnesses consist of poorly functioning brain regulatory mechanisms that produce distressing symptoms, upsetting and ineffective actions, and some degree of voluntary impairment.[56]

- They are diseases of the mind and body.

- They involve disturbances of mood, thinking, and behavior.

- They include a failure of vegetative functioning, e.g., sleep, sex drive, and appetite.

ANOREXIA NERVOSA

Definition of the Illness

Anorexia nervosa is the semi-starvation of a person from self-induced food restriction. It is a potentially life-threatening medical condition causing serious damage to major organs. Many of the signs and symptoms are those associated with starvation. Obsessive compulsive features are often present that may or may not involve food. The clients appear physically emaciated. They achieve weight loss by vomiting, abusing laxatives or excessive exercising. Illogical fear of weight gain and distorted perception of self-image and body are common in this disease.

Median Age of Onset

Commonly begins during adolescence or young adulthood. It rarely begins before puberty, or after age forty, but there are examples of both of these extremes.[57]

Risk Factors

Individuals who have obsessive compulsive traits and/or anxiety disorders are at risk. People who live in a culture where thinness is valued or where they are engaged in occupations which include modeling and athletics would also be at risk. Anorexia is most prevalent in post-industrialized, high-income countries such as the United States, Europe, Australia, New Zealand, and Japan.[58]

Prevalence of anorexia nervosa is comparatively low among Latinos, African Americans, and Asians in the United States. Another risk is having a first-degree biological relative with the disorder.

General Considerations

Treatment teams should include inpatient and outpatient therapy. Team members should consist of registered dietitians (RDs), a certified eating-disorder-registered dietitian, and a board-certified specialist in eating disorders. Other team members in treatment would include psychiatrists and psychologists. Therapists also should be knowledgeable and caring. Support group leaders, especially peer support leaders, also have their place.

- The therapeutic milieu should consist of Inpatient Treatment, Residential Treatment, Partial Hospitalization (PHP), Intensive Outpatient (IOP), Extended Day Treatment, and Transitional Living.
- Pastoral counseling is beneficial and can involve pastor's wives and women in the church, especially those who have had eating disorders.

A pastor and the client's family are important to assure follow-through with the treatment of the person with anorexia. They can help ensure that if a person leaves a treatment center, there has been communication between the inpatient and outpatient programs.

Persons with this disorder may feign compliance with treatment. They may be told, for example, not to exercise as part of their therapy, and it has been discovered that they are indeed exercising. They may have been asked about specific food consumption, and then were found to be cheating in that regard. They may feel they are in complete control because they are not eating, when they are truly out of control when it comes to eating, drinking, and exercising. They need structure ,and they also need empathy.

Tips for the Pastor

When your member comes to see you about this issue of anorexia, you should talk openly and honestly and take the time to listen. Remember that eating disorders are not about the food. Know your limits; be patient. Don't try to be a therapist. Don't be afraid of upsetting them; speak up. Don't say, "Just eat and get over it." Don't threaten them with consequences or bully them. As a pastor, be aware of the services in your area. Disciple men not to be critical toward women and their weight, but encourage the men and young men to put a premium on inner beauty. "Charm is deceitful and beauty is vain, but a woman who fears the Lord, she shall be praised" (Prov. 31:30). The answers to eating disorder questions are not yes or no; eating disorder issues are much more complex, and their severity is on a continuum.

Referral Protocol

Community resources may be gleaned from others around you, on the Internet, or through the United Way. There are independent mental health programs of which you should be aware. I would encourage you to find out about Christian treatment facilities in your area online and through referrals. This is a serious problem and it is not getting better by itself. These men and women are another part of your flock that needs your care.

ATTENTION-DEFICIT HYPERACTIVITY DISORDER (ADHD)

Definition of the Illness

Attention-Deficit Hyperactivity Disorder is a common neurological disorder, present in both children and adults. It is estimated that between three and five percent of children have attention-deficit problems. Symptoms can include inattention, difficulty staying focused, feelings of restlessness, and difficulty controlling behavior.

Median Age of Onset

In general, a child shouldn't receive a diagnosis of attention-deficit/hyperactivity disorder unless the core symptoms of ADHD start early in life—before age twelve—and create significant problems at home and at school on an ongoing basis.

ADHD has three subtypes[59]

Predominantly inattentive

Children with this subtype are less likely to act out or have difficulties getting along with other children. They may sit quietly, but they are not paying attention to what they are doing. Therefore the child may be overlooked, and parents and teachers may not notice that he or she has ADHD.

Six of the following symptoms must be present:

- Fails to give close attention to details or makes careless mistakes in schoolwork, work, or other activities
- Has difficulty sustaining attention in tasks or play activities
- Does not seem to listen when spoken to directly
- Does not follow through on instructions and fails to finish schoolwork, chores, or duties in the workplace (not due to oppositional behavior or failure to understand instructions)
- Has difficulty organizing tasks and activities
- Avoids, dislikes, or is reluctant to engage in tasks that require sustained mental effort (such as schoolwork or homework)

- Loses things necessary for tasks or activities (e.g., toys, school assignments, pencils, books, or tools)
- Easily distracted by extraneous stimuli

Predominantly hyperactive-impulsive
- Most symptoms (six or more) are in the hyperactivity-impulsivity categories
- Fewer than six symptoms of inattention are present, although inattention may still be present to some degree

At least six of the following signs of hyperactivity-impulsivity must apply:

Hyperactivity
- Fidgets with hands or feet or squirms in seat
- Leaves seat in classroom or in other situations in which remaining seated are expected
- Runs about or climbs excessively in situations in which it is inappropriate (in adolescents or adults, may be limited to subjective feelings of restlessness)
- Has difficulty playing or engaging in leisure activities quietly
- Appears "on the go" or acts as if "driven by a motor"
- Talks excessively

Impulsivity
- Blurts out the answers before the questions have been completed
- Has difficulty waiting turn
- Interrupts or intrudes on others (e.g., butts into conversations or games)
- Some hyperactive-impulsive or inattentive symptoms that caused impairment were present before age seven
- Some impairment from the symptoms is present in two or more settings (e.g., at school [or work] and at home)
- There must be clear evidence of clinically significant impairment in social, academic, or occupational functioning
- The symptoms do not occur exclusively during the course of a pervasive developmental disorder or other psychotic disorder, and are not better accounted for by another mental disorder (e.g., mood disorder, anxiety disorder, dissociative disorder, or a personality disorder)

Combined hyperactive-impulsive and inattentive
- Six or more symptoms of inattention and six or more symptoms of hyperactivity-impulsivity are present.
- Most children have the combined type of ADHD.

Risk factors for attention-deficit/hyperactivity disorder may include:
- Blood relatives, such as a parent or sibling, with ADHD or another mental health disorder
- Exposure to environmental toxins—such as lead, found mainly in paint and pipes in older buildings
- Maternal drug use, alcohol use, or smoking during pregnancy
- Premature birth[60]

Treatment Options

Currently available treatments focus on reducing the symptoms of ADHD and improving functioning. Treatments include medication, various types of psychotherapy, education, or training, or a combination of treatments. Treatments can relieve many of the disorder's symptoms, but there is no cure. With treatment, most people with ADHD can be successful in school and lead productive lives. Researchers are developing more effective treatments and interventions, and using new tools such as brain imaging, to better understand ADHD and to find more effective ways to treat and prevent it.

General Considerations

ADHD can be mistaken for other problems Parents and teachers can miss the fact that children with symptoms of inattention have the disorder because they are often quiet and less likely to act out. They may sit quietly, seeming to work, but they are often not paying attention to what they are doing. They may get along well with other children, compared with those with the other subtypes, who tend to have social problems. But children with the inattentive kind of ADHD are not the only ones whose disorders can be missed. For example, adults may think that children with the hyperactive and impulsive subtypes just have emotional or disciplinary problems.

Tips for the Pastor

Pastors should be supportive of parents who have a child with ADHD. Pastors should be careful not to undermine the treatment, as many so-called "biblical counselors" do. This makes the problem more difficult. A great place to get information on the web is at Health Central (http://www.health-central.com/ADHD).

Referral Protocol

While treatment won't cure ADHD, it can help a great deal with symptoms. Treatment typically involves medications and behavioral interventions. Early diagnosis and treatment can make a big difference in outcome.

AUTISM SPECTRUM DISORDER

Definition of the Illness

Autism spectrum disorder (ASD) is the name for a group of developmental disorders. ASD includes a wide range—a "spectrum"—of symptoms, skills, and levels of disability. Restrictive/repetitive behaviors may include:

- Repeating certain behaviors or having unusual behaviors
- Having overly focused interests, such as with moving objects or parts of objects

Median Age of Onset

The age and pattern of onset also should be noted for autism spectrum disorder. Symptoms are typically recognized during the second year of life (12–24 months of age) but may be seen earlier than twelve months if developmental delays are severe, or noted later than 24 months if symptoms are more subtle.[61]

Risk Factors

Scientists do not know the exact causes of ASD, but research suggests that genes and environment play important roles.

According to the *Diagnostic and Statistical Manual of Mental Disorders* (DSM–5), the best-established prognostic for individual outcomes with autism within the spectrum disorder is presence or absence of associated intellectual disability and language impairment (e.g., functional language by age five years) and additional mental health problems. Epilepsy, as a comorbid diagnosis, is associated with greater intellectual disability and lower verbal activity.

A variety of nonspecific risk factors, such as advanced parental age, low birth weight, or fetal exposure to valproate, may contribute to the risk of autism spectrum disorder.[62]

Boys are more likely to be diagnosed with ASD than girls. Other predictive factors include:

- Having a sibling with ASD
- Having *older parents* (a mother who was thirty-five or older, and/or a father who was forty or older, when the baby was born)

- Genetics—about twenty percent of children with ASD also have certain genetic conditions. Those conditions include Down syndrome, fragile X syndrome, and tuberous sclerosis, among others.[63]

Treatment Options

Early treatment for ASD and proper care can reduce individuals' difficulties while helping them learn new skills and make the most of their strengths. The very wide range of issues facing those "on the spectrum" means that there is no single best treatment for ASD. Working closely with a doctor or health care professional is an important part of finding the right treatment program. There are many treatment options, social services, programs, and other resources that can help.

General Considerations

A doctor may use medication to treat some difficulties that are common with ASD. With medication, a person with ASD may have fewer problems with:

- Irritability
- Aggression
- Repetitive behavior
- Hyperactivity
- Attention problems
- Anxiety and depression

Tips for the Pastor

Groups targeting parents of children with autism or on the autism spectrum can be found in most communities, as well as some churches. Parents need support, so referral to these support systems is important. As a pastor, be aware that your children's ministry staff needs training, compassion, and patience when it comes to children with special needs. These children can feel cornered when directly confronted. Giving a "time out" will probably not yield the desired outcome. Remember that these parents need your preaching and the fellowship of other believers, which puts their children under the care of your teachers. Try to stress to children's workers that an unhappy child produces an unhappy parent who may not return. These children are little sheep who need wise and loving care.

Referral Protocols

- A developmental pediatrician—a doctor who has special training in child development
- A child psychologist and/or child psychiatrist—a doctor specially educated in brain development and behavior

BIPOLAR DISORDER

There are four basic types of bipolar disorder; all of them involve clear changes in mood, energy, and activity levels. These moods range from periods of extremely up, elated, and energized behavior (known as manic episodes) to very sad, down, or hopeless periods (known as depressive episodes). Less severe manic periods are known as hypomanic episodes.

Bipolar I disorder, formerly known as manic-depressive illness, is a brain disorder that causes unusual cycles in mood, energy, and activity levels. It is an affective disorder characterized by extreme changes of heightened energy, creativity and social ease contrasted by depression, poor self-esteem, inability to feel pleasure, and suicidal ideation. Without treatment, these can escalate out of control in mood from manic to depressive states.

Sometimes, a person with severe episodes of mania or depression also has psychotic symptoms (bipolar psychosis), such as hallucinations or delusions. The psychotic symptoms tend to match the person's extreme mood. For example:

- Someone having psychotic symptoms during a manic episode may believe she is famous, has a lot of money, or has special powers.
- Someone having psychotic symptoms during a depressive episode may believe he is ruined and penniless, or that he has committed a crime.
- As a result, people with bipolar disorder who also have psychotic symptoms are sometimes misdiagnosed with schizophrenia.

Bipolar Mixed States (also called Mixed Mania or Rapid Cycling)
Bipolar mixed states is a period during which symptoms of a manic and a depressive episode are present at the same time. People who experience mixed states describe feeling activated and "revved up," but are also full of anguish and despair. Rapid, pressured speech can coexist with impulsive, out-of-control full of anguish and despair. Rapid, pressured speech can co-exist with impulsive, out-of-control thoughts of suicide, self-destruction, or aggression. Hopelessness, irritability, uncontrollable swings between racing thoughts, and a feeling of "being in blackness" can all happen over the course of minutes.

Definition of the Illness

Bipolar II disorder is defined by a pattern of depressive episodes and hypo-manic episodes, but not the full-blown manic episodes described above. A person with this disorder generally cycles faster into a depressive episode, which is different in one who is major depression recurrent.

Median Age of Onset

Although bipolar disorder can occur at any point in life, the average age of onset is twenty-five. Every year, 2.9% of the U.S. population is diagnosed with bipolar disorder, with nearly eighty-three percent of cases being classi-fied as severe. Bipolar disorder affects men and women equally.

Risk Factors

- **Genetics:** Some research suggests that people with certain genes are more likely to develop bipolar disorder than others. But genes are not the only risk factor for bipolar disorder. Studies of identical twins have shown that even if one twin develops bipolar disorder, the other twin does not always develop the disorder—despite the fact that identical twins share all of the same genes.

- **Family History:** Bipolar disorder tends to run in families. Children with a parent or sibling who has bipolar disorder are much more likely to develop the illness, compared with children who do not have a family history of the disorder.

Treatment Options

Since bipolar disorder is a complex disease, it is suggested that a person see a psychiatrist. He will also need to have pastoral counseling, since the disorder has severe mania and depression and often the family does not know what to do. For some people, it may be appropriate to have a psychologist evaluate and test the client and recommend therapy.

Christians who are afflicted with bipolar disorder must be assured that this sickness is part of God's providential ordering. People who are bipolar generally seek help when they are in the depressive phase of the illness.

General Considerations for Bipolar Disorder

We need to make sure that a family member or caregiver is in the first meet-ing that the client has with a psychiatrist, so they can give accurate informa-tion about the person's history of symptoms of mind, mood and behavior, which includes a substance abuse history. Many psychiatrists have therapists who will gather facts about the client, before his meeting with the psychia-trist. This meeting should also have someone who can help to differentiate between, fact and fiction.

Tips for the Pastor

Bipolar disorder, as with all the mental illnesses, begs for community. Hopefully your church has a support group. At Heartfelt Counseling Ministries/CAMI, we help people start support groups in churches and other places of ministry. We have written curriculum for the groups to follow. The groups need to address both families and the person suffering from bipolar disorder. A person with this disorder may resist going to the group because of paranoia, stigma, fear of self-disclosure, and other reasons. Many parents and spouses will come even if the sufferer does not come.

Referral Protocols

The Internet will be helpful in finding a psychiatrist. Many psychiatrists have therapists in their office who help especially with gathering data, family history, and the reason for your visit. As a pastor, you might volunteer to go with the client to see the psychiatrist. Often, when one is in a mental health crisis, he is not a good historian; therefore, it is advisable that a family member or friend attend the appointment. Pastoral counseling is vital for people with bipolar disorder.

Bipolar and Children

Bipolar disorder is not the same as the normal ups and downs every kid goes through; bipolar symptoms are more powerful than that. The mood swings are more extreme and are accompanied by changes in sleep, energy level, and the ability to think clearly. Bipolar symptoms are so strong that they can make it hard for a child to do well in school, or get along with friends and family members. The illness can also be dangerous. Some young people with bipolar disorder try to hurt themselves or attempt suicide. Children and teens with bipolar disorder should get treatment. With help, they can manage their symptoms and lead successful lives.

Bipolar "mood episodes" include unusual mood changes along with unusual sleep habits, activity levels, thoughts, or behavior. In a child, these mood and activity changes must be very different from their usual behavior and from the behavior of other children.

Children and teens having a manic episode may:

- Feel very happy or act silly in a way that's unusual for them and for other people their age
- Have a very short temper
- Talk really fast about a lot of different things
- Have trouble sleeping but not feel tired
- Have trouble staying focused
- Talk and think about sex more often
- Do risky things

Children and teens having a depressive episode may:

- Feel very sad
- Complain about pain a lot, such as stomach aches and headaches
- Sleep too little or too much
- Feel guilty and worthless
- Eat too little or too much
- Have little energy and no interest in fun activities
- Think about death or suicide

At the present time, there is no cure for bipolar disorder. Doctors often treat children who have the illness in much the same way they treat adults. Treatment can help control symptoms. Steady, dependable treatment works better than treatment that starts and stops.

Erikson's stages of psycho-social development, as articulated by Erik Erikson in collaboration with Joan Erikson, is a comprehensive psychoanalytic theory that identifies a series of eight stages in which a healthy developing individual should pass through, from infancy to late adulthood.[64]

BORDERLINE PERSONALITY DISORDER

Definition of the Illness
Borderline Personality Disorder (BPD) is a serious mental disorder marked by a pattern of ongoing instability in moods, behavior, self-image, and functioning. These incidents often result in impulsive actions and unstable relationships. A person with BPD may experience intense episodes of anger, depression, and anxiety that may last from only a few hours to days.

Medium Age of Onset
Symptoms usually occur first in the teenage years and early twenties. However, onset may occur in some adults after the age of thirty.

Risk Factors
Neglectful parenting and repeated physical, emotional, and sexual abuse are very common environmental risk factors. Also, a dysfunctional family of origin who fails to validate the individual's personhood without offering solutions to their suffering is a common risk for these emotional victims.

Treatment Options
Dialectical Behavior Therapy (DBT) is done with a team of therapists who meet every week to discuss cases. A support group should be led by two of the therapists who meet once a week for ninety minutes. Individual psychotherapy should be done weekly with the same therapist to ensure continuity of care. For mindfulness skills, and if the treatment center is in a Christian setting, you can focus on Old Testament wisdom literature, i.e., Job, Psalms, Proverbs as well as the sayings of Christ. This includes the study of biblical meditation and contemplation. There is a hierarchy of targets in DBT. This involves decreasing suicidal, therapy-interfering, and/or quality-of-life behaviors.

General Considerations
I believe, as a therapist and a Christian leader, that Christians in the mental health profession should make it a priority to know the Bible and theology, in order to lay a good foundation for his or her training in the mental health arena.

Normally, a psychiatrist is part of the team. Sometimes these clients have co-occurring disorders such as major depression, post-traumatic stress disorder, and obsessive compulsive disorder. A psychiatrist must help diagnose these people and prescribe medications for disorders previously mentioned.

The teaching of behavioral skills is very important in this treatment. The basic skills are core mindfulness skills, interpersonal effectiveness skills, distress tolerance skills, and emotional regulation skills. BPD is made up of five groups of symptoms: unstable behavior, unstable emotions, unstable relationships, unstable sense of identity, and awareness problems.

Tips for the Pastor

Dr. Marsha Linehan is the leading authority in treating BPD. People who suffer from this emotional disorder have historically been very difficult to treat, and therefore difficult to help. Dr. Linehan developed a theory that has been used with a tremendous amount of success when applied correctly. I was personally trained by her at the University of Washington in Seattle and saw the programs implemented successfully in the community Mental Health agency where I worked for years. I have also adapted her programs in my own practice. Dr. Linehan does not believe in absolute truth, but as a Christian I know that the Bible is inerrant and God-breathed (2 Tim. 3:16). In my opinion, mindfulness skills in the United States have turned into a humanistic way of dealing with stress, and goes beyond what Linehan intended for a skill needed within the treatment of borderline personality disorder. Mindfulness has actually become a sort of religion.

The typical client is a female (although I have treated males) who has been sexually abused and suffers from post-traumatic stress disorder (PTSD). These individuals have difficulty regulating their emotions; in fact, Linehan calls them "emotional burn victims." They have fear of abandonment and chaotic relationships, and therefore they are deregulated interpersonally. They have serious self-esteem issues and usually allow others to define who they are. They have an unstable sense of self and a sense of emptiness. Behavioral deregulations are characterized by self-injury and impulsive behaviors such as substance abuse and promiscuity. Cognitive deregulation is indicated by paranoia and dissociative responses, which are made worse by stressful situations.

Dysregulations in any of these areas occur when a person with BPD is out of control, not simply upset. Through the skills learned in Dialectical Behavior Therapy, clients can learn to better control all of these areas by taking a step back, being more mindful, analyzing what works, and acquiring new behaviors.

Emotional dysregulation is viewed as a joint outcome of biological disposition, environmental context, and the transaction between the two during development. The theory asserts that borderline individuals have difficulties in regulating several, if not all, emotions. The systemic dysregulation is produced by emotional vulnerability and by maladaptive and inadequate emotion modulation strategies.[65]

Referral Protocols

In DBT, a therapist does not have to have a master's degree. Linehan's emphasis for a skilled behavioral therapist is that he or she is one who has the temperament to deal with those who have BPD. In some cases, staff including a psychologist or LCSW (Licensed Clinical Social Worker) should lead the team, to fulfill the requirements of insurance companies and the United States government.

BULIMIA NERVOSA

Definition of the Illness

Bulimia nervosa is a psychological and severe life-threatening eating disorder defined by the ingestion of an abnormally large amount of food in a short time period, followed by an attempt to avoid gaining weight by purging what was consumed. Methods of purging include forced vomiting, excessive use of laxatives or diuretics, and extreme or prolonged periods of exercising. Often, in these binge/purge episodes, a woman or man suffering with this disorder will experience a loss of control and engage in frantic efforts to undo these feelings.[66]

Median Age of Onset

Bulimia nervosa commonly begins in adolescence or young adulthood. Onset before puberty or after age forty is uncommon. The binge eating frequently begins during or after an episode of dieting or losing weight. Experiencing multiple stressful life events also can precipitate an onset of bulimia nervosa.

Risk Factors

- Temperamental: Weight concerns, low self-esteem, depressive symptoms, social anxiety disorder, and overanxious disorder of childhood are associated with increased risk of development of bulimia nervosa.
- Environmental: Internalization of a thin body ideal has been found to increase risk for developing weight concerns, which in turn increase risk for the development of bulimia nervosa. Individuals who experienced childhood physical or sexual abuse are also at risk for developing bulimia nervosa.
- Genetic and physiological: Childhood obesity and early puberty; familial transmission of bulimia nervosa may be present, as well as genetic vulnerabilities for the disorder.

Treatment Options

Most places that deal with anorexia and bulimia use the same treatment modalities and mental health professionals. There are a number of Christian programs in the United States.

General Considerations

Both anorexia nervosa and bulimia are characterized by an overvalued drive for thinness and a disturbance in eating behavior. The main difference between diagnoses is that anorexia nervosa is a syndrome of self-starvation, involving significant weight loss of fifteen percent or more of ideal body weight, whereas patients with bulimia nervosa are, by definition, at normal weight or above. Bulimia is characterized by a cycle of dieting, binge-eating, and compensatory purging behavior to prevent weight gain. Purging behavior includes vomiting, and diuretic or laxative abuse. When underweight individuals with anorexia nervosa also engage in binging and purging behavior, the diagnosis of anorexia nervosa supersedes that of bulimia.

Tips for the Pastor

See "Tips for the Pastor" under Anorexia Nervosa.

Referral Protocols

See "Referral Protocols" under Anorexia Nervosa.

CHILDHOOD DEPRESSION

Definition of the Illness

A clinical depression includes negative thinking, especially about self-worth, depressed mood (which may be great sorrow, fear, down in the dumps, or simply not feeling well). It is typified by low energy levels and a lack of interest in otherwise pleasurable activities. Existing along a spectrum, this mental state can range from mild to severe, with suicidal thoughts/actions being a possibility on the severe end of the spectrum. Depression can be found in all age groups; however, symptoms of childhood depression vary from adult depression.

Median Age of Onset

Depression can occur as early as four to five years old, and those in adolescence can not only suffer severe depression but also successfully commit suicide. It is a leading cause of health impairment (morbidity) and death (mortality). About three thousand adolescents and young adults die by suicide each year in the United States, making it the third leading cause of death in people ten to twenty-four years of age.

General Considerations

Children may suffer from episodes of moderate to severe depression associated with depressive disorder, or more chronic (mild to moderate) low mood of dysthymia. Depression may also be part of other mood disorders like bipolar disorder, as a result of psychosis (for example, symptoms of delusions or hallucinations); as part of a medical condition like hypothyroidism; or the result of exposure to certain medications such as cold medications. Teen depression would not need an antipsychotic medication, as long as the phases of bipolar disorder do not include psychosis from a something like cocaine withdrawal.

Risk Factors

Depression in children does not have one specific cause. Rather, children or teens with this illness tend to have a number of biological, psychological, and environmental contributors. Biologically, depression is associated with a deficient level of the neurotransmitter serotonin. Some of the areas in the brains of teens and children are smaller, and there is also increased activity in different parts of their brains than in adults.

There is thought to be at least a partially genetic component to the patterns of children and teens. Children with a depressed parent are as much as four times more likely to develop the disorder. Children who have depression or anxiety are more prone to have other biological problems, i.e., low birth weight, trouble sleeping, or having a mother younger than eighteen years old at the time of their birth.

Psychological contributors to depression include low self-esteem, negative body image, being excessively self-critical, and often feeling helpless when dealing with negative events.

Children who suffer from conduct disorder, attention deficit hyperactivity disorder (ADHD), clinical anxiety, cognitive or learning problems, or trouble engaging in social activities also are more at risk of developing depression.

Depression may be a reaction to life stresses or some type of trauma, including verbal, physical, or sexual abuse; the death of a loved one; school problems; being bullied; or peer pressure. Youth who are struggling to adapt to American culture have also been found to be at higher risk for depression. Other contributors include poverty and financial difficulties in general, exposure to violence, social isolation, parental conflict, divorce, and other causes of disruptions to family life. Children who have limited physical activity or poor school performance are also at a greater risk.

Treatment Options
Due to the societal stigma that can be associated with receiving mental health treatment, pediatricians and other primary care doctors are often the first professionals approached for diagnosis and treatment of depression.

General Considerations
Childhood depression often results in the child being unable to perform daily activities, such as getting out of bed or getting dressed, performing well at school, or playing with peers. Children with depression may also experience the classic symptoms of a mood disorder, but may exhibit other symptoms as well, including, impaired performance of schoolwork, persistent boredom, quickness to anger, and frequent physical complaints like headaches and stomach aches. They participate in more risk-taking behaviors than normal and show less concern for their own safety. Examples of risk-taking behaviors in children include unsafe play, like climbing excessively high or running in the street.

Abandoned Child Syndrome was common in Romania and Russia when babies were left alone in their cribs, ignored, and neglected for the first few years of life except to be changed or fed. The Bucharest Project[67] in 2000 studied children who had been abandoned in 1989 when the Romanian dictator Nicolae Ceausescu was overthrown. David Wolfe and Kathryn Hildyard made similar observations in a 2002 study: "The list of problems that stem from neglect reads like the index of the DSM: poor impulse control, social withdrawal, problems with coping and regulating emotions, low self-esteem, pathological behaviors such as tics, tantrums, stealing and self-punishment, poor intellectual functioning and low academic achievement."[68]

Parents of children with depression often report the following behavior changes in the child:

- Crying more often or more easily
- Increased sensitivity to criticism or other negative experiences
- More irritable mood than usual or compared to others their age and gender, leading to vocal or physical outbursts, or defiant, destructive, angry, or other acted-out behaviors
- Irregular eating and sleeping patterns, significant increase or decrease in weight change, or failure to achieve appropriate weight gain for their age
- Unexplained physical complaints (e.g., headaches or abdominal pain)
- Social withdrawal; the youth spends more time alone, away from friends and family
- Overly pessimistic, hopeless, helpless, excessively guilty feelings, or a feeling of worthlessness
- Statements about hurting himself or herself, or engaging in reckless or other potentially harmful behavior.

Depression is associated with a number of other mental health conditions, such as attention deficit hyperactivity disorder (ADHD), autism-spectrum disorders, bipolar disorder, post-traumatic stress disorder (PTSD), and anxiety disorders, so the evaluator will look for signs and symptoms of manic depression (bipolar disorder), a history of trauma, and other mental health symptoms. Childhood depression also may be associated with a number of medical problems, or it can be a side effect of various medications, exposure to drugs, of abuse or other toxins.

Tips for the Pastor

Remember that the Lord Jesus is called a Wonderful Counselor (Isa. 9:6). He rebuked his disciples for not allowing the little children come to him. Pastoral counseling is very important for children who suffer from childhood depression. They need hope, encouragement, and help when the environment is too powerful for them. You should try to find a Christian psychiatrist in your area. Heartfelt Counseling Ministries can help you with this. If a child has witnessed a terrorist attack, a serious car accident, lives in a war zone, or has been a part of a natural disaster, he will probably need therapy for PTSD.

Referral Protocol

Many health care providers can help determine if the diagnosis of clinical depression is appropriate in children, including licensed mental health counselors, pediatricians, and other primary care providers, specialists seen for a medical problem, emergency room doctors, psychiatrists, psychologists, psychiatric nurses, nurse practitioners, physician assistants, and social workers.

DYSTHYMIC DISORDER

Definition of the Illness
Dysthymic disorder (or dysthymia) is characterized by chronic low-level depression. While the depression is not as severe as that characterizing major depressive disorder, a diagnosis of dysthymia requires having experienced a combination of depressive symptoms for two years or more. Dysthymic disorder affects approximately 1.5 percent of the adult population in the United States.[69]

A number of people who have a chronic dysthymic disorder have a major depression that is super imposed on the dysthymia. When the major depression is treated it usually leaves, but many people still have the persistent depression or dysthymia. One must be careful of the situation where the untreated major depression is considered dysthymia.

Median Age of Onset
"Early and gradual onset in childhood, adolescence, or early adult life and by definition, a chronic course."[70]

Risk Factors
Childhood risk factors include loss of parents or separation from parents.

Treatment Options
This diagnosis is somewhat complex; it is therefore often undiagnosed. It is a subset of Major Depression Disorder. A mental health professional should be contacted to help with this diagnosis.

General Considerations
It is sometimes assumed that because dysthymia is not as severe as some depressions, it can't be treated by medications. This is not true, and one should be careful not to imply that the person has not learned how to successfully handle stress.

Tips for the Pastor
See "Tips for the Pastor" under Major Depression Disorder.

Referral Protocol
Psychological testing would be helpful, as well as seeing a psychiatrist.

GENERALIZED ANXIETY DISORDER

Definition of the Illness
Generalized Anxiety Disorder (GAD), which affects 6.8 million adults or 3.1 percent of the US population, is characterized by persistent and excessive worry about a number of different things. Individuals with GAD may worry more than seems warranted about actual events, or may expect the worst even when there is no apparent reason for concern.

Median Age of Onset
The median age of onset of GAD is thirty years, though the actual onset is spread over a larger range. Symptoms may occur earlier, but onset of disorder rarely occurs before adolescence.

Risk Factors
Women are twice as likely to have the disorder as men. Specific factors include people who have been diagnosed with major depression disorder and other types of mental illness; people who are perfectionists; those who have had severe trauma, such as the loss of a child.

"Individuals of European descent tend to experience generalized anxiety disorder more frequently than do individuals of non-European descent, i.e., Asian, African, Native American and Pacific Islander. Further, individuals from developed countries are more likely than individuals from non-developed countries to report that they have experienced symptoms that meet criteria for generalized anxiety disorder in their lifetime."[71]

Treatment Options
This disorder needs cognitive therapy. Some practitioners treat clients with benzodiazepines (tranquilizers), but these are addictive drugs and should only be used for the short term. The better drugs which have been a proven help are SSRIs, which we have mentioned repeatedly for treating faulty brain chemistry. Sometimes a specific traumatic event can trigger this disorder and if so, that should be addressed in therapy.

GAD diagnosis is somewhat controversial in its treatment. Many pastors and counselors feel that anxiety is only a sin problem, and that Philippians 4:6–7 is the answer for dealing with an anxiety diagnosis:

> Be anxious for nothing, but in everything by prayer and supplication with thanksgiving let your requests be made known to God. And the peace of God, which surpasses all comprehension, will guard your hearts and your minds in Christ Jesus.

This is a wonderful passage. However, the problem is two-pronged:

1) Pastors often preach this passage with great gusto, because somewhere they have used this formula and it has worked.

2) The Bible tells us, "If Christ is in you, though the body is dead because of sin, yet the spirit is alive because of righteousness" (Rom. 8:10). The body is our mortal body, not the fleshy sin nature. Our body includes the brain. For some reason, there are some people whose brains are susceptible to worry or thinking there is going to be a disaster. They have muscle tension and fatigue. They worry about work. They have extreme test anxiety, if in school. They have feelings that they will get in an accident or that their plane will crash. This is not normal. It comes from faulty brain chemistry. These are people whom the Bible calls "small souled" and they should be comforted.

> We urge you, brethren, admonish the unruly, encourage the fainthearted, help the weak, be patient with everyone (1 Thess. 5:14).

General Considerations

God is in every tomorrow,
Therefore I live for today;
Certain of finding at sunrise
Guidance and strength for the day,
Power for each moment of weakness,
Hope for each moment of pain
Comfort for every sorrow,
Sunshine and joy after rain.
God is in every tomorrow,
Planning for you and for me,
Even in the dark I will follow,
Trust where my eyes cannot see,
Stilled by His promise of blessing
Soothed by the touch of His hand
Confident in His protection,
Knowing my life-path is planned.

—Laura A. Barter Snow

Tips for the Pastor

Charles Jefferson spoke about the importance of "leading the sheep":

> It is commonplace that a minister is a leader, and yet not every minister knows how to lead. In other words, he is not a good pastor. Some ministers try to drive. Their fatal weakness is an inability to see that shepherds cannot drive. Such men are always cutting, lashing, forcing, and therefore always getting into trouble. They are continually quarreling with their people, and for no other reason than that they do not know how to lead. They push and do not draw, they shove and do not woo. They believe in propulsion and not in attraction. They lack the magic of the shepherd touch.[72]

Referral Protocol

A good place to start would be to talk to a pastor. The pastor should be skilled and compassionate when dealing with anxiety. If there is a need for medications, a primary doctor or a psychiatrist should be consulted.

ILLNESS ANXIETY DISORDER

Definition of the Illness
Illness anxiety disorder, sometimes called hypochondriasis or health anxiety, is worrying excessively that you are or may become seriously ill. One may have no physical symptoms, or believe that normal body sensations or minor symptoms are signs of severe illness, even though a thorough medical exam doesn't reveal a serious medical condition.

Median Age of Onset
Onset of illness anxiety disorder usually occurs during early or middle adulthood.

Risk Factors
Risk factors for illness anxiety disorder may include:

- A major life stress
- Threat of a serious illness which is nothing serious
- History of abuse as a child
- A serious childhood illness or a parent with a serious illness
- A personality that includes being a worrier
- Excessive health-related Internet use

Treatment Options
Antidepressants, such as selective serotonin reuptake inhibitors (SSRIs), may help treat illness anxiety disorder. Medications to treat mood or anxiety disorders, if present, also may help. Cognitive behavioral therapy has been found to be useful in the treatment of this illness.

General Considerations
There is some disagreement among experts about the definition and treatment of this disorder. The DSM–4 used the category of hypochondriasis, but not the DSM–5. The International Classification of Diseases (ICD) also has some disagreement with the DSM–5.

Tips for the Pastor

A pastor is needed to "encourage the fainthearted" (1 Thess. 5:14b), using Scriptures of encouragement, especially those concerning the providence of God and His working out His plan in one's life, such as:

> Come now, you who say, "Today or tomorrow we will go to such and such a city, and spend a year there and engage in business and make a profit." Yet you do not know what your life will be like tomorrow. You are just a vapor that appears for a little while and then vanishes away. Instead, you ought to say, "If the Lord wills, we will live and also do this or that" (James 4:13–15).

Referral Protocols

Some experts tie in this disorder with other anxiety disorders, especially the obsessive compulsive disorders and other "related disorders" (OCD/RD). Part of this treatment also includes the sufferer's personal physician, a psychiatrist, and a therapist. A pastor is also needed to help the "small souled."

A good place to start would be to talk to a pastor. The pastor should be skilled and compassionate when dealing with anxiety. If there is need for medications, a primary doctor or psychiatrist should be consulted.

MAJOR DEPRESSION DISORDER

(CLINICAL DEPRESSION, ENDOGENOUS DEPRESSION, BIOLOGICAL DEPRESSION)

Definition of the Illness
Major depression is an affective disorder characterized by a depressed mood most of the day, especially in the morning and loss of interest and a failure to appreciate activities or relationships that were formerly enjoyable. Symptoms can also include disturbances of a person's vegetative functions—those necessary to sustain life—such as having little or no appetite or increased appetite, a low sex drive, and severe sleep disturbances, which one professor of psychiatry called the "litmus test of endogenous depression."[73] Poor concentration, feelings of hopelessness, worthlessness and guilt, suicidal thoughts, mental deadness, psychomotor agitation, or psychomotor retardation are also usually present, making this a very serious disorder.

Median Age of Onset
Major depression can occur at any age, but often begins in adulthood

Risk Factors
Depression is one of the most common mental disorders in the US. Current research suggests that depression is caused by a combination of genetic, biological, environmental, and psychological factors. Some experts believe that the first episode comes as a result of stress. (See the Appendix D: The Holmes-Rahe Scale.) Personal or family history of depression, major life changes, trauma, stress, certain physical illnesses, and medications can all be a part of worsening this disorder.

Treatment Options
Antidepressants and some mood stabilizers are the mainstays of treatment. Supportive counseling and cognitive therapy can be part of an effective treatment. It is important that you link your client with a mental health professional, especially if their depression is severe. You will need to encourage a person that the medicines will work, but that it takes time.

General Considerations

Most antidepressants take at least two weeks to work, and sometimes more. A basic rule of psychiatry is that the psychiatrist, after initial dosing, will gradually increase the amount of the medication until the symptoms are alleviated or the side effects become intolerable. He often will begin a new medication or add another medication to the mix.[74] People should not change their medication dosages, etc., without discussion with the physician.

Tips for the Pastor

It is important that suicidal assessment be done when dealing with a person who has major depression. Fifteen percent of those who have the disorder will successfully kill themselves. Some of those who suffer from this disorder will need help in monitoring and setting up their medications. Please see appendix for suicidal assessment tools, as well as the chapter on Suicide.

Referral Protocol

In some cases a primary physician is able and willing to prescribe antidepressants. For the more complex depressions, a psychiatrist should be consulted. Supportive pastoral counseling is essential. Mental health professionals can also be a source for therapy. Some individuals with severe and persistent mental illnesses will need case management.

OBSESSIVE-COMPULSIVE DISORDER

Definition of the Illness
Obsessive-compulsive disorder (OCD) is an anxiety disorder characterized by recurrent, unwanted thoughts (obsessions) and/or repetitive behaviors (compulsions). Repetitive behaviors such as hand washing, counting, checking, or cleaning are often performed with the hope of preventing obsessive thoughts or making them go away. They spend at least one hour a day on these thoughts and rituals, which cause distress and get in the way of daily life. Performing these so-called "rituals," however, provides only temporary relief, and not performing them markedly increases anxiety. OCD is not a personality disorder.

Median Age of Onset
Approximately 2.2 million American adults age eighteen and older, or about one percent of the population, have OCD. It strikes men and women in roughly equal numbers and usually appears in childhood, adolescence, or early adulthood. A subgroup of OCD patients, a majority of them male, have symptom onset in childhood. Some childhood-onset OCD may have a different clinical course and a different underlying neurobiology than adult-onset OCD.[75]

Risk Factors
Twin and family studies suggest that there is a genetic susceptibility of OCD. In addition, this genetic vulnerability may be greater in pediatric onset, since there is greater heritability in this population. One-third of adults with OCD develop symptoms as children, and research indicates that OCD might run in families.[76]

Treatment Options
Like many other anxiety disorders, OCD is treated by serotonin selective reuptake inhibitors (SSRIs) such as Zoloft, Paxil, Celexa, and Lexapro, along with cognitive behavioral therapy.

General Considerations
OCD is often called the "silent disease." This is because some of the images that come to the mind may be embarrassing to the individual. This diagnosis

is not a violent one. The client is not "hearing command voices to kill." Symptoms of OCD may come and go, and be better or worse at different times. Compulsions are not performed with the primary purpose of deriving pleasure, although some individuals experience relief from anxiety that accompanies the compulsive behavior as pleasurable.

"OCD has significant comorbidity with other psychiatric illnesses, particularly, major depressive disorder, other anxiety disorders, and Tourette's disorder. Notably, there is evidence that OCD patients with comorbid tic disorder may be a biologically distinct entity with earlier age of onset."[77]

Tips for the Pastor

The client should be able to tell you about his thoughts. You should be able to handle whatever they say. Focus on the ritual first. Behavioral therapy should help diminish the rituals. Pastors should be aware that Christians who have this disorder cannot distinguish between temptation and sin. He must be told that the Holy Spirit is not a "nag." He should ask God to search his heart, as did the psalmist when he prayed:

> Search me, Oh, God and know my heart; try me and know my anxious thoughts; and see if there is any hurtful way in me, and lead me in the everlasting way (Ps. 139:23–24).

Besides asking God to search his heart, he needs to understand the theology of temptation and sin.

> Let no one say when he is tempted, "I am being tempted by God"; for God cannot be tempted by evil, and He Himself does not tempt anyone. But each one is tempted when he is carried away and enticed by his own lust. Then when lust has conceived, it gives birth to sin; and when sin is accomplished, it brings forth death. Do not be deceived, my beloved brethren (James 1:13–16).

Referral Protocols

Unless a clinician, doctor, or a pastor asks the right questions, OCD will likely go undetected. If your member shows signs of abnormally repetitive actions, for example, excessive hand washing, straightening and re-straightening items, checking for his own pulse, or doubting actions which he has clearly already taken, he should be assessed by a mental health professional.

PANIC DISORDER

Definition of the Illness
Panic disorder (PD) attacks are characterized by a fear of disaster or of losing control even when there is no real danger. A person may also have a strong physical reaction during a panic attack. He may feel like he is having a heart attack. Panic attacks can occur at any time, and many people with panic disorder worry about the possibility of having another attack.

Median Age of Onset
"Age of onset varies for this disorder, but it is generally between late adolescence and the mid-30s."[78]

Risk Factors
Twin studies have indicated that familial risk is particularly elevated for first-degree relatives of those who developed PD prior to age twenty. Researchers have found that several parts of the brain, as well as biological processes, play a key role in fear and anxiety.

Treatment Options
As with other anxiety disorders, panic disorder is usually treated with SSRIs and cognitive behavior therapy.

General Considerations
People with panic attacks regularly have the symptoms below:

- Emotional and behavioral
  - Sudden and repeated attacks of fear
  - A feeling of being out of control during a panic attack
  - A fear or avoidance of places where panic attacks have occurred in the past
  - An intense worry about when the next attack will occur
- Physical
  - Pounding or racing heart
  - Sweating
  - Breathing problems
  - Weakness or dizziness

- Feeling hot or a cold chill
- Tingly or numb hands
- Chest pain
- Stomach pain

Tips for the Pastor

About one in three people with panic disorder develops *agoraphobia*, a condition in which the individual becomes afraid of being in any place or situation where escape might be difficult or help unavailable in the event of a panic attack.

Referral Protocols

It is often reassuring to recommend to the client that he see a primary physician who can order blood tests or other diagnostics to rule out disease or disorders. If the person receives a good report, he should be discouraged from continually seeing the doctor. Instead he should be referred to a psychiatrist, who will prescribe an appropriate antidepressant.

PERINATAL DEPRESSION

Definition of the Illness
Perinatal depression is a depression that occurs during pregnancy or within a year after delivery. Researchers believe that depression is one of the most common complications during and after pregnancy.

Risk Factors
Factors that may increase the likelihood of depression during or after pregnancy can include: history of depression or substance abuse and family history of mental illness with previous pregnancy or birth. Hormonal changes and changes in body weight normally occur during and after pregnancy, but these symptoms may also be signs of depression.[79]

Treatment Options
The treatment of perinatal depression is more complicated than major depression disorder. A woman who suffers from this disorder, as well as the baby, are both important pieces of the perinatal treatment. There are some restrictions regarding pregnant women and the prescribing of antidepressants. More health providers are needed to treat this disorder.

General Considerations
Some women, from the beginning, need to be helped with insurance and possible Medicaid assistance. Both mother and baby need proper nutrition during and after pregnancy, and the WIC (Women, Infants, and Children) program in the United States will also help. The depression for these women may be so severe that they fear being pregnant ever again. The future may bring more discoveries in the efficacy of treatment for pregnant women with depression.

Tips for the Pastor
The best scenario for a woman who suffers from this disease would be to connect with an older woman who has had perinatal depression. Pastors should realize the seriousness of this very real disorder, and be sensitive to these suffering new moms. The mothers also experience guilt for their lack of attachment toward their new baby. Their husbands need to be educated and assisted through these episodes, because depression is truly a family disease. Help with

the baby, occasional meals, calls of support and housekeeping assistance are all practical ways to help her in her depression. During the pregnancy or if she is breastfeeding, decisions have to be made about medications.

Unfortunately, postpartum depression is quite common, with ten to fifteen percent of women experiencing it.[80]

Women usually begin to experience postpartum depression within the first two weeks after childbirth. However, symptoms may not appear for up to one year after childbirth.

Referral Protocols
A woman suffering from perinatal depression should consult her OB/GYN, who may refer her to a psychiatrist for an evaluation and treatment.

Postpartum Psychosis
Another form of perinatal depression is postpartum psychosis. Postpartum psychosis is a serious illness that can be severe and life-threatening. The psychotic symptoms include delusions (thoughts that are not based in reality), hallucinations (hearing or seeing things that aren't there) or disorganized thinking. Often mothers who develop postpartum psychosis are having a severe episode of a mood disorder, usually bipolar (manic-depression) disorder with psychotic features. It is essential for women to get evaluation and treatment immediately.[81] For crisis or emergency situations, please call UNC Crisis Psychiatry at (919) 966-2166.

POST-TRAUMATIC STRESS DISORDER (PTSD)

Definition of the Illness

The Anxiety and Depression Association of America defines PTSD as follows: "A serious potentially debilitating condition that can occur in people who have experienced or witnessed a natural disaster, serious accident, terrorist incident, sudden death of a loved one, war, violent personal assault such as rape, or other life-threatening events."[82]

Median Age of Onset

While PTSD can occur at any age, the average age of onset is in a person's early twenties.[83]

Risk Factors

Serious road accidents, violent personal assaults, sexual, mugging or robbery; prolonged sexual abuse, violence or severe neglect, witnessing violent deaths, military combat, being held hostage, terrorist attacks, natural disasters, diagnosis of a life-threatening illness, unexpected severe injury, death of a close family member or friend, or a severe mental illness episode. PTSD isn't usually related to situations that are simply upsetting, such as divorce, job loss, or failing exams.

PTSD develops in about one in three people who experience severe trauma. It isn't fully understood why some people develop the condition while others don't. However, certain factors appear to make some people more likely to develop PTSD.

If you've had depression or anxiety in the past, or you don't receive much support from family or friends, you're more susceptible to developing PTSD after a traumatic event.[84]

General Considerations

PTSD affects 3.5% of the US adult population—about 7.7 million Americans—but women are more likely to develop the condition than men. About thirty-seven percent of those cases are classified as severe. The symptoms of PTSD fall into the following categories:

- Intrusive Memories, which can include flashbacks of reliving the moment of trauma, bad dreams, and scary thoughts.
- Avoidance, which can include staying away from certain places or objects that are reminders of the traumatic event. A person may also feel numb, guilty, worried, or depressed or have trouble remembering the traumatic event.
- Dissociation, which can include out-of-body experiences or feeling that the world is "not real" (derealization).
- Hypervigilance, which can include being startled very easily, feeling tense, trouble sleeping, or outbursts of anger.[85]
- The DSM–5 has pertinent information about post-traumatic stress disorder in preschool children.[86]

Tips for the Pastor

Use comforting passages from the Bible to help those with PTSD. Many of these can be found in the Old Testament wisdom literature (e.g., Job, Psalms, Proverbs, Ecclesiastes). It would be wise to use caution in your sermons, that you don't make any jokes regarding anyone suffering from PTSD. People with PTSD often have "apparent competence," when actually they are a "bundle of nerves."

PREMENSTRUAL DYSPHORIC DISORDER (PMDD)

Definition of the Illness
Premenstrual dysphoric disorder (PMDD) is a severe form of premenstrual syndrome (PMS). Like PMS, premenstrual dysphoric disorder follows a predictable, cyclic pattern. Symptoms begin in the late luteal period (the period in the menstrual cycle that follows ovulation).

Median Age of Onset
PMDD can occur at any point after the menarche (the first occurrence of menstruation).

Risk Factors
Risk factors for this disorder include stress, history of interpersonal trauma, seasonal changes and sociocultural aspects of female sexual and female gender role in particular. Genetic and physiological heritability of premenstrual dysphoric disorder is unknown.[87]

Treatment Options
Seventy-five percent of women report relief of symptoms when treated with SSRIs; in randomized controlled trials, the only birth control pills that have reflected improvement in PMDD symptoms are Yaz, Ocella, and Beyaz. These medications have been shown to offer relief from both physical and psychological PMDD symptoms, with improvement in health-related quality of life.

Anyone benefits from a whole and nutritious diet. Women with PMDD stand to benefit even more. Studies show a strong correlation between what we eat and emotional well-being. A common symptom of PMDD is an intense craving for food during the luteal phase, specifically foods high in carbohydrates, and with good reason: Carbohydrates influence the production of serotonin, which directly and indirectly controls mood, sexual desire and function, appetite, sleep, memory, body temperature, and social behavior.

General Considerations
"Brain areas that regulate emotion and behavior are studded with receptors for estrogen, progesterone, and other sex hormones. These hormones affect the

functioning of neurotransmitter systems that influence mood and thinking — and in this way may trigger PMDD. But it's not clear why some women are more sensitive than others. Genetic vulnerability likely contributes.

"Other risk factors for developing PMDD include stress, being over-weight or obese, and a past history of trauma or sexual abuse. Antidepres-sants that slow the reuptake of serotonin provide effective treatment for premenstrual dysphoric disorder (PMDD). These drugs alleviate PMDD more quickly than depression, which means that women don't necessarily have to take the drugs every day. Hormone therapies provide additional options, but are generally considered second-line treatments."[88]

Tips for the Pastor

Pastors should try to be sympathetic toward the women in their church who suffer these symptoms. It is a serious issue for many women, and instructing them to "calm down" or "be more disciplined" is not the right message. The women who present with this disorder need sympathetic counseling, and perhaps medical referral to treat it.

Referral Protocols

The most logical place to start if a woman has these symptoms is her OB/GYN or her primary care physician, who may refer the patient to a psychia-trist, if necessary.

SCHIZOAFFECTIVE DISORDER

Definition of the Disorder

Schizoaffective disorder is a condition which includes chronic symptoms of schizophrenia, combined with episodes of an affective disorder (either bipolar or depressive). Signs and symptoms of schizoaffective disorder may include, among others:

- Delusions, having false, fixed beliefs
- Hallucinations, such as hearing voices
- Major depressed mood episodes
- Possible periods of manic mood or a sudden increase in energy and behavioral displays that are out of character
- Impaired occupational and social functioning
- Problems with cleanliness and physical appearance[89]

The exact cause of schizoaffective disorder is not known. A combination of factors may contribute to its development, such as:

- Genetic links
- Brain chemistry
- Brain development delays or variations
- Exposure in the womb to toxins or viral illness, or even birth complications

Risk Factors

- Factors that increase the risk of developing schizoaffective disorder include having a close biological (blood) relative who has:
  - Schizophrenia
  - Bipolar disorder
  - Schizoaffective disorder
- Complications—people with schizoaffective disorder are at an increased risk of:
  - Social isolation
  - Unemployment
  - Anxiety disorders
  - Developing alcohol or other substance abuse problems

- Significant health problems
- Suicide

Suicidal Thoughts or Behavior

Expression of suicidal thoughts or behavior may occur in someone with schizoaffective disorder. If you have a loved one who is in danger of committing suicide or has made a suicide attempt, make sure someone stays with that person. Call 911 or your local emergency number immediately. Or, if you think you can do so safely, take the person to the nearest hospital emergency room.

If you think someone you know may have schizoaffective disorder symptoms, talk to that person about your concerns. Although you can't force someone to seek professional help, you can offer encouragement and support, and help your loved one to find a qualified doctor or mental health provider.

SCHIZOPHRENIA

Definition of the Illness

Schizophrenia is a chronic, disabling brain disease. Its symptoms include delusions, thoughts of being controlled, and a blunted or inappropriate affect. (Affect in this sense refers to one's expression of emotion as demonstrated through facial expression, tone of voice or body language.[90]) Symptoms also include disorganized thoughts, and grossly disorganized or catatonic behavior. Other indicators of the disease are a scarcity of thoughts (alogia), thought broadcasting, an overall loss of interest (volitional), and "auditory hallucinations in which either a voice keeps up a running commentary on the patient's behavior or thoughts as they occur or two or more voices conversing with each other."[91]

Median Age of Onset

Men tend to develop schizophrenia slightly earlier than women; whereas most males become ill between sixteen and twenty-five years old, most females develop symptoms several years later, and the incidence in women is noticeably higher after age thirty.

Risk Factors

Scientists have observed that schizophrenia can run in families; but this is not always true. Scientists also think that interactions between genes and aspects of the individual's environment are necessary for schizophrenia to develop. Environmental factors may involve:

- Exposure to viruses
- Malnutrition before birth
- Problems during birth
- Psychosocial factors

Treatment Options

Doctors and patients can work together to find the best medication, dosage, or medication combination. Learn the basics about stimulants and other mental health medications on the NIMH: Mental Health Medications webpage; and check the FDA website (www.fda.gov) for the latest information on warnings, patient medication guides, and newly approved medications.

General Considerations

1. Positive symptoms are unusual thoughts or perceptions, including auditory and visual hallucinations, delusions, and disorders of movement. Some people with schizophrenia believe that they can broadcast what they are thinking into another person's mind. Others have the false belief (delusion) that they are being controlled by someone else.

2. Negative symptoms represent a loss or a decrease in the ability to initiate plans, speak, express emotion, or find pleasure in everyday life. These symptoms are harder to recognize as part of the disorder and can be mistaken for laziness or depression.

3. Cognitive symptoms (or cognitive deficits) are problems with attention, certain types of memory, and the executive functions that allow us to plan and organize.[92]

Tips for the Pastor

A key portion of Scripture regarding this specific mental illness is found in 1 Samuel 21:13–15:

> So he disguised his sanity (*ta`am*, which means judgment) before them, and acted insanely (*halal*, to act like a madman) in their hands, and scribbled on the doors of the gate, and let his saliva run down into his beard. Then Achish said to his servants, "Behold, you see the man behaving as a madman (*shaga*) Why . . . have you brought this one to act the madman (shaga) in my presence?"

David's ruse of insanity corresponds with conceptual disorganization, which is a part of schizophrenia.

There is some confusion about schizophrenia and demon-possession. They are not the same. There are some similarities, but even more differences.

Referral Protocol

People with this disease need hands-on help. One thing to do would be to connect the person with a case management program. You or someone in your church needs to be a CAMI advocate.

SEASONAL AFFECTIVE DISORDER (SAD)

Definition of the Illness

Seasonal affective disorder (SAD) is characterized by the onset of depression during the winter months, when there is less natural sunlight. This depression generally lifts during spring and summer. Winter depression, which is typically accompanied by social withdrawal, increased sleep, and weight gain, predictably returns every year in a seasonal affective disorder:

- Sleep problems occur, usually a desire to oversleep. But sometimes sleeplessness and early wakening can be symptoms.
- Lethargy is common, a feeling of fatigue, and inability to carry out a normal routine.
- Sufferers tend to overeat, craving carbohydrates and sweets. This naturally results in weight gain.
- Some people with SAD have joint and body aches and pain.[93]

Median Age of Onset

Onset usually occurs between eighteen and thirty years of age. Since this is a subset of major depression, also see Major Depression Disorder.

Risk Factors

- SAD is diagnosed four times more often in women than men.
- It is extremely rare for anyone who lives within thirty degrees of the Equator.
- People with a family history of other types of depression are more likely to develop SAD than people who do not have a family history of depression.
- If a person has depression or bipolar disorder, the symptoms of depression may worsen with the seasons (but SAD is diagnosed only if seasonal depressions are the most common).
- Younger adults have a higher risk of SAD than older adults. SAD has been reported even in children and teens.

Treatment Options

SAD can be treated by natural sunlight, or by a light which generates ten thousand lux. It is a good idea is to have an eye exam before you starting this treatment for this class of depression. Other treatments include Vitamin D, and antidepressants.

General Considerations

Some people will have a hard time with this diagnosis, but it is a true disorder. My wife, Robyn, had SAD when we lived in Grand Rapids, Michigan. She grew up in Florida with continual sunshine. But any time we moved north, she suffered from Seasonal Affective Disorder. I bought her a ten-thousand lux light, which she used every morning in the fall and winter for twenty years. It made quite a difference in her overall outlook. Her energy came back, she was not feeling depressed, and she didn't crave carbs.

Tips for the Pastor

There may be some people in your church who do not know about SAD; they may even have it every year and not understand why they feel like they do. The Internet is a good source for finding a suitable SAD light; if you have members without Internet access, someone could offer to help them locate a light. If the price is prohibitive, maybe the church could buy one and let members share it.

SEPARATION ANXIETY

Definition of the Illness
For a diagnosis of separation anxiety disorder, a clinician looks for distress in being separated from—or anticipating separation from—parents or caregivers which would be considered excessive for the child's age, and prevents him from participating in age-appropriate activities. Symptoms include worry about losing parents or other attachment figures through illness or death; unreasonable fear of an event that causes separation (getting lost, or being kidnapped); reluctance or refusal to leave home for school; undue fear of sleeping or being alone; persistent nightmares about separation; and physical symptoms (headaches, stomach aches) in conjunction with separation or anticipation of separation. To meet the criteria for separation anxiety disorder, the child must have the symptoms for over two weeks.

Median Age of Onset
Separation anxiety disorder occurs in children of at least six years old.

Risk Factors
Separation anxiety appears to be heritable, but it is often triggered by stress, trauma, or changes in environment, such as a move to a new home or school or a death or divorce in the family. Separation anxiety may occur later in life as the form of panic disorder.

Treatment Options
Behavioral therapy and supportive psychotherapy will help those with this disorder, as well as antidepressants.

The parents should be brought into the overall treatment. Medication should also be prescribed to alleviate a child's distress and facilitate therapy. A variety of medications have been shown to be effective in treating separation anxiety disorder; the first-line medication is one of the SSRIs (selective serotonin reuptake inhibitor family).

General Considerations
As with the other disorders, separation anxiety has its roots in biology, not faulty parenting. Our daughter, Lindsay, suffered from this disorder beginning in the fourth grade. We know the frustration of trying to coax a child to

school. The former chair of psychiatry at the University of Kansas warned us not to get her into long-term therapy, which has actually bankrupted parents. Lindsay was prescribed medication by a child psychiatrist, and we conducted our own behavior therapy, which gradually resulted in her successful return to school.

Schools should be made aware of the situation and be monitored in the way they treat the child who has this disorder, although there has been improvement in the general sense. Students may complain of headaches, stomach aches, and other gastro-intestinal problems.

Tips for the Pastor
The child and his parents should know that the pastors of the church will support them. Youth pastors need to be open to helping the children through youth activities, especially summer and winter camps.

Referral Protocol
Some children do well with therapy by a school counselor or another children's therapist. Some will need to be seen by a psychiatrist.

SOCIAL ANXIETY DISORDER

Definition of the Illness
People with social anxiety disorder (sometimes called "social phobia") have a marked fear of social situations or when they are expected to perform. They expect to feel embarrassed, judged, rejected, or fearful of offending others.

Risk Factors
Researchers are finding that genetic and environmental factors, frequently in interaction with one another, are risk factors for anxiety disorders. Specific factors include:

- Shyness, or behavioral inhibition, in childhood
- Being female
- Having few economic resources
- Being divorced or widowed
- Exposure to stressful life events in childhood and adulthood
- Anxiety disorders in close biological relatives
- Parental history of mental disorders
- Elevated afternoon cortisol levels in the saliva (specifically for social anxiety disorder)

Treatment Options
Two specific stand-alone components of cognitive behavior therapy used to treat social anxiety disorder are cognitive therapy and exposure therapy.

Cognitive therapy focuses on identifying, challenging, and then neutralizing unhelpful thoughts underlying anxiety disorders. Exposure therapy focuses on confronting the fears underlying an anxiety disorder in order to help people engage in activities they have been avoiding, and is used along with relaxation exercises and/or imagery. Meta-analysis, which pulls together previous studies and calculates the statistical magnitude of the combined effects, found that cognitive therapy was superior to exposure therapy for treating social anxiety disorder.

General Considerations
After you meet with your parishioner and decide to refer her to a therapist or other health care professional, get her permission, then direct her to ask the

professional for a release of information form, stating "I, _____, consent to a release of information to Pastor _____."

Tips for the Pastor

It is good to help guide someone with social anxiety disorder to visit places where he will have successful social interactions. Everyone is not created the same; sometimes a person just needs some gentle encouragement to make progress. We are to love and encourage one another, in order to minister.

We must also realize that there are negative life events which can trigger a person with the right (or wrong) neurobiology into a full-blown disorder. Things that may seem insignificant to us may be insurmountable to them. A simple greeting in a department store, or trying to work at a job where person-to-person interaction is expected, may cause your client major angst.

As a pastor-teacher, the days of feeling nervous speaking in front of a crowd are probably well in your past—but it is not so with those who have social anxiety. In a similar way, every Christian has a spiritual gift; some are serving gifts, and some are speaking gifts. Moses stands as a great example of a man who at one time was strong and independent until he spent forty years in the wilderness. When God called him to speak to Pharaoh, he refused many times because he had become insecure about his abilities. He said of himself:

> Please, Lord, I have never been eloquent, neither recently nor in time past, nor since You have spoken to Your servant; for I am slow of speech and slow of tongue (Exod. 4:10).

Yet, Stephen said of him:

> Moses was educated in all the learning of the Egyptians, and he was a man of power in words and deeds (Acts 7:22).

SUBSTANCE ABUSE-DUAL DIAGNOSIS

Definition of the Illness

Addiction is the state of being enslaved to a habit or practice, or to something that is psychologically or physically habit forming (such as alcohol, narcotics, cannabis, cocaine and heroin), to such an extent that stopping causes extreme trauma. My concern in this book is to communicate the way substance abuse affects the mentally ill mind.

Dual Diagnosis (Substance Abuse with Mental Illness)

Mental illness is frequently accompanied by addictive, futile attempts at "self-medication," but the two things have to be treated separately. In treatment, the connection of mental illness with substance abuse is called a "dual diagnosis." Especially if they aren't getting good health treatment, persons are drawn to substances that cause them to feel better (for a while). Depressants such as alcohol, barbiturates, or marijuana—or stimulants such as speed, dexedrine, or cocaine—can help alleviate some symptoms, or just help the person forget problems associated with the mental illness.

One gravitates to a drug that gives the effect opposite to the symptom of the mental condition. Someone with mania tends toward alcohol dependency. A depressive is drawn to abuse "uppers" or speed. These and other medications affect the central nervous system and either release or block dopamine in the brain. Hallucinogens radically alter brain chemistry, promising freedom and pleasure, but giving only worse depression or agitation as they wear off.

In a previous book (*Broken Minds: Hope for Healing When You Feel like You're Losing It*) my wife Robyn and I covered many types of mental illness. In the appendix, we discussed substance abuse. A number of medical doctors, therapists, and mental health professionals emailed me and questioned my stance on substance abuse and sin. When I asked if they looked up the Scriptures that I gave, they almost all said, "I did not."

This is really a matter of truthfulness and biblical inerrancy. Galatians 5:19–21 says, "Now the deeds of the flesh [sinful nature] are evident, which are . . . drunkenness, carousing, and things like these, of which I forewarn you, just as I have forewarned you, that those who practice such things will not inherit the kingdom of God."

The word *drunkenness* here means intoxication. Notice that Paul does not intend to provide an exhaustive list, for he adds "and things like these." *Carousing* covers behaviors associated with intoxication, such as sexual immorality, aggression, recklessness, and whatever else one does while self-control is lost. The words are used together elsewhere, as in Romans 13:13: "Let us behave properly as in the day, not in carousing and drunkenness."

Median Age of Onset

Age of onset would be anywhere from ten years of age to high school. There are also a number of people who will start abusing substances when they have symptoms of a mental illness that interfere with their mood, thought and behavior.

Risk Factors

Here is a quote from the United States Assistant Secretary for Mental Health and Substance Abuse: "I have often found that my psychiatric practice's patients diagnosed with depression, bipolar disorder or another mental illness also were living with untreated drug or alcohol problems. The presence of both substance abuse and mental illness is known as a co-occurring disorder. Left untreated, this condition poses a serious threat to an individual's quality of life, including increased risk of family problems, frequent drug relapse, numerous hospitalizations, unemployment, homelessness, serious physical illness and death. This is an important public health challenge. In 2016, more than 8 million American adults struggled with co-occurring disorders, including 2.5 million who had a serious mental illness such as schizophrenia, bipolar disorder or major depression. Many more are undiagnosed. Less than half of those living with co-occurring disorders are getting treatment. It is critical that we get the message out: Early detection and treatment can improve outcomes and quality of life for those with co-occurring disorders."[94]

Treatment Options

Treatment can be difficult for a person who has a dual diagnosis. If they are intoxicated and also have major depression, the tendency of detoxification units is to say that they are not trained to handle problems with mental illness, especially if the person is having suicidal thoughts. On the other hand, many psychiatric hospitals will not deal with alcohol problems. To further complicate matters, there are many drug rehabilitation treatment programs that will not allow antidepressants or other drugs for mental illness to be part of the program. This includes therapists who wish to only use cognitive therapy or cognitive behavioral therapy. This is a problem, because eliminating the psychotropic medications will cause the client to relapse; the many positive steps that he made will be lost, and the cycle will repeat.

General Considerations

The best treatment program—whether it is outpatient, partial hospitalization, or inpatient—will understand and treat both the addiction and the mental illness. The caregiver or some other person (sometimes the pastor) needs to ensure that the patient will get the right treatment. It often takes an addict to know another addict, and a treatment program will have therapists who "have been there."

Pastoral counselors have greater freedom to bring Scripture to bear on addictions than do believers who work as secular drug and alcohol counselors; but the abstinence principles found in secular programs have enough foundational truth that they will help even those who do not wish to bow the knee to Christ. A counselor must be discerning, whether working in or out of a Christian context, to deal effectively with those who are guilty of substance abuse.

Assure the client that you understand the problem, and that you are able to get the help he or she needs. Show confidence in directing him or her knowing your support will be comforting. (You can make calls, or do Internet searches and explore the options later). Your member/client has probably thought about this meeting with you for a long time, and he or she needs to feel your unconditional love and acceptance. Use the shepherd model: Seek the lost sheep, and bind up what is broken. Find a suitable treatment program that addresses dual diagnosis. For some it will be local; for others, being away from his or her atmosphere of using may be a better choice. The choice would also depend on insurance coverage, ability to travel, etc.

Referral Protocols
SAMSHA has a mental health treatment center "locator." Enter a zip code, and your nearest facility will be shown. There is also other helpful information on their website: https://findtreatment.samhsa.gov.

SUICIDE

ADULT AND TEEN

Adult

Suicide is often the result of, but not limited to the following affective disorders: bipolar mania and bipolar depression; major depression, perinatal, (sometimes called postpartum depression disorder), and schizoaffective disorder and we find it especially present in borderline personality disorder.

Suicide in the United States has surged to the highest levels in nearly thirty years, with increases in every age group except older adults. The rise was particularly steep for women. It was also substantial among middle-aged Americans, sending a signal of deep anguish from a group whose suicide rates had been stable or falling since the 1950s. The suicide rate for middle-aged women, ages forty-five to sixty-four, jumped by sixty-three percent over the period of the study, while it rose by forty-three percent for men in that age range, the sharpest increase for males of any age. The overall suicide rate rose by twenty-four percent from 1999 to 2014, according to the National Center for Health Statistics. The increases were so widespread that they lifted the nation's suicide rate to thirteen per 100,000 people, the highest since 1986. The rate rose by two percent a year starting in 2006, double the annual rise in the earlier period of the study. In all, 42,773 people died from suicide in 2014.[95] The current suicide rate for veterans is more than twenty per day.

I am no stranger to the temptation of suicide. In a previous book, *Broken Minds: Hope for Healing When You Feel Like You're Losing It*, which I co-authored with my wife Robyn, I tell the story of my own suicidal ideation and plans. I was spared that heinous act by God and by His grace alone, I didn't attempt it. But the psychic pain of my deep depression was so severe that I must say, I considered it. I was on a self-imposed suicide watch with my family and friends. I walked and prayed short, desperate prayers while I began the exhausting search for an antidepressant that would take away my depression.

My sister, Cindy, who also inherited the bipolar gene, bought twenty of our books and gave them to some of her friends and our cousins. She read it and knew that she and I both suffered from this mental affliction. Yet, in 2006, she took her own life in the midst of a depressive episode.

The Elephant in the Room

Suicide is a subject about which very few speak. It is also the hidden death in the obituary. So and so "died suddenly" or "unexpected" are usually the terms that cloak the painful truth.

It happens all the time. If you don't believe that, just look at the statistics that opened this chapter. Some people shrink from discussing it, feeling almost superstitiously afraid of the topic or believing that they will put the idea into someone's head. Believe me, if your loved one or church member is suffering from a depressive illness, he has already thought of suicide and probably has a plan. If you broach the subject, you will not be leading him to that end. You will have the opportunity to tell him you will find him help and you will support him until he gets well again.

Suicide is like a plague that moves through communities killing its victims one by one and those who seem immune to it ignore the possibility of death until it takes someone they love. Then it becomes a dangerous adversary. But instead of attacking it head-on, we hide it from the others who are susceptible. Why do we continue to disguise ourselves or our friends and family members as cheery and buoyant when they are woefully depressed? Because we believe it is a character flaw to be depressed? Because we don't honestly believe it is a biological disease? Well, it is, and it is happening to our sons and daughters, to our children and our parents. We need to talk about it, stop the shaming and blaming, and get help for anyone who is experiencing this illness before it is too late.

"Just Say No" Won't Work

Between the nature of the disease and the devil himself, we face formidable obstacles to keep living; to continue on in that anguish is overwhelming. Suicides are complex because they involve biological, chemical imbalances, and strong and clever satanic attacks. Never underestimate the power of the enemy.

Pastor, do we have a seminar for you! We can train your staff and other groups in your church to be aware of this epidemic. In our book *Broken Minds* I wrote the following acrostic, which I use in my practice:

Severe depressive symptoms must be relieved.

Unconditional Love should be shown to the suicidal person.

Interventions are in order, such as obtaining lethal means of suicidal people, implementing a detailed treatment plan if necessary, which includes getting them effective medications or possibly ECT.

Cries for help should be attended to—not ignored. These cries may be verbal or could be actions that a suicidal person takes to be noticed.

Intoxication of drugs and alcohol impairs judgment and loosens inhibitions, which make it easier for the suicidal person to take his/her life.

Deliberate planning by a person contemplating suicide should be identified. Sometimes psychiatric hospitalization is required.

Exhortation needs to be done by a fellow believer, urging the suicidal person not to buy into demonic deception or submit to the devil who appears as a roaring lion.[96]

Common warning signs for suicide include:

- Making suicidal statements
- Being preoccupied with death in conversation, writing, or drawing
- Giving away belongings
- Withdrawing from friends and family
- Having aggressive or hostile behavior
- Saying a subtle goodbye in a letter, phone call, or in person

It is extremely important that you take all threats of suicide seriously and seek immediate treatment for your child or teenager. If you are a child or teen and have these feelings, talk with your parents, an adult friend, or your doctor right away and get help!

Other warning signs can include:

- Neglecting personal appearance
- Running away from home
- Risk-taking behavior, such as reckless driving or being sexually promiscuous
- A change in personality (such as from upbeat to quiet)

Pastors and primary physicians are often the first and last person to counsel a suicidal person. Here are some tips for a pastor who meets with a person who is contemplating suicide:

1. Don't start off by asking them if they want to commit suicide. Show them that you care, and that you can help them with their problems.

2. Check the indicators that show that a person is in a severe depression—disturbances of sleep, or loss of appetite which includes weight loss and gastrointestinal problems. Also ask them about their sex drive.

3. Ask them if they are depressed.

4. Ask them to tell you on a scale of one to ten (without using the number 5) how bad their depression is.

5. Ask them if they hear voices.

6. Ask if there is a history of depression or mental illness in their family.

7. Ask if they hear voices and whether or not it is a running conversation between two people, a voice criticizing them, or a voice commanding them to hurt or kill someone.

8. Ask them if they have a plan, and how close are they to carrying it out.

9. Ask them if they have direct contact to lethal means—for example, a gun, a rope in the trunk, or some sort of poison. If they do, ask them if they plan to use those means and whether they would give those items to you.

10. Ask them what kind of medications (or drugs) they take.

11. If they don't have a psychiatrist, ask them if they need help finding one.

12. If they are considering suicide and have a plan, tell them that you think they should consider putting themselves in the hospital.

13. If they are hearing command voices and are in danger to hurt or kill themselves, they need to be hospitalized.

14. If they are psychotic and hearing command voices to hurt or kill someone else, you should refer them to psychiatric hospital for a mental evaluation.

Suicide is a very important subject for a pastor to consider. There are also cases of pastors committing suicide every year. Suicides occur every day in the world in which we live; in fact, many physicians and mental health professionals commit suicide.

SUICIDAL THOUGHTS AND SUICIDE ATTEMPTS

Teens and Suicide Risk
Certain problems increase the chances of suicidal thoughts in children and teens. Problems that increase the chances of suicidal thoughts include:

- Depression or another mental health problem, such as bipolar disorder (manic-depressive illness) or schizophrenia

- A parent with depression or substance abuse problems
- Previous attempts at suicide
- A friend, peer, family member, or hero (such as a sports figure or musician) who recently attempted or died by suicide
- A disruptive or abusive family life
- A history of sexual abuse
- A history of being bullied

Problems that may trigger a suicide attempt in children and teens include:

- Possession or purchase of a weapon, pills, or other means of inflicting self-harm
- Drug or alcohol use problems
- Witnessing the suicide of a family member
- Problems at school such as falling grades, disruptive behavior, or frequent absences
- Loss of a parent or close family member through death or divorce
- Legal or discipline problems
- Stress caused by physical changes related to puberty, chronic illness, and/or sexually transmitted infections
- Withdrawing from others and keeping thoughts to themselves
- Uncertainty surrounding sexual orientation

Key facts

- Every year close to 800,000 people take their own life and there are many more people who attempt suicide. Every suicide is a tragedy that affects families, communities and entire countries, and has long-lasting effects on the people left behind.

- Suicide occurs throughout the lifespan and was the second leading cause of death among 15–29-year-olds globally in 2015.

- Suicide does not just occur in high-income countries, but is a global phenomenon in all regions of the world. In fact, over 78% of global suicides occurred in low and middle-income countries in 2015.

- Suicide is a serious public health problem; however, suicides are preventable with timely, evidence-based and often low-cost interventions. For national responses to be effective, a comprehensive multi-sectoral suicide prevention strategy is needed.

Who is at risk?

While the link between suicide and mental disorders (in particular, depression and alcohol use disorders) is well established in high-income countries, many suicides happen impulsively in moments of crisis with a breakdown in the ability to deal with life stresses, such as financial problems, relationship break-up, or chronic pain and illness.

In addition, experiencing conflict, disaster, violence, abuse, loss, and a sense of isolation are strongly associated with suicidal behavior. Suicide rates are also high amongst vulnerable groups who experience discrimination, such as refugees and migrants; indigenous peoples; lesbian, gay, bisexual, transgender, intersex (LGBTI) persons; and prisoners. By far the strongest risk factor for suicide is a previous suicide attempt.[97]

Scripture tells us that the devil is very interested in self-murder. Jesus spoke about the nature and the practice of the devil to the Pharisees:

> You are of your father the devil, and you want to do the desires of your father. He was a murderer from the beginning, and does not stand in the truth because there is no truth in him. Whenever he speaks a lie, he speaks from his own nature, for he is a liar and the father of lies (John 8:44).

Our Lord further showed the nature of Satan and the power of God when he was dealing with a demon-possessed son, whose father and mother had watched the results of the possession all his life. When the Lord Jesus asked his father how long his son had this demon, he said:

> From childhood. It has often thrown him both into the fire and into the water to destroy him (Mark 9:21–22b).

The demons wanted to kill the child, and while "Legion" (the consortium of demons in him) possessed him, he was tormented and suffered in both body and spirit.

What is often overlooked is that suicide has a spiritual side. Pastor, you should be trained in suicide assessment. Yes, we know that *the battle belongs to the LORD*. However, this does not mean that churches should just "let go and let God," when its members come up against suicide. In your church, you should have a suicide hotline. The pastors should be trained in suicide awareness and stop-gap interventions. The devil is a very intelligent being. He knows more Scripture than we do. He takes advantage of the hopelessness and the horrible psychic pain of depression and he is merciless.

Suicide leaves children in its wake who will practice the act like the parents who model it. It is a fact that most people will not commit suicide the first time they try it. Each time a person attempts suicide, it weakens his or her resolve to live. It is necessary that training be done for pastors in suicide awareness, and prevention. At Heartfelt Counseling Ministries, we offer training for pastors and others who need it.

COMMON QUESTIONS ABOUT MENTAL ILLNESS

1. What is impaired awareness of an illness?

Impaired awareness of illness (anosognosia) means that the person does not recognize that he or she is sick. The person believes that their delusions are real (e.g., the woman across the street really is being paid by the CIA to spy on him or her) and that their hallucinations are real (i.e., the voices really are instructions being sent by the president).

2. What can I do when someone has a mental illness, but does not think they are sick or need treatment?

Impaired awareness of an illness is a major problem, because it is the single largest reason why individuals with schizophrenia and bipolar disorder do not take their medications. It is caused by damage to specific parts of the brain, especially the right hemisphere.

Many studies of individuals with schizophrenia report that approximately half of them have moderate or severe impairment in their awareness of illness. Studies of bipolar disorder suggest that approximately forty percent of individuals with this disease also have impaired awareness of illness. This is especially true if the person with bipolar disorder also has delusions and/or hallucinations. When taking medications, awareness of illness improves in some patients.

Anosognosia is a strange thing. It is difficult to understand how a person who is sick would not realize, it and it is very difficult for other people to comprehend. To other people, a person's psychiatric symptoms seem so obvious that it's hard to believe the person is not aware that he or she is ill. It is not only difficult, it is impossible for patients with certain right-hemisphere singularly difficult, for even the most sensitive observer, to picture the inner state, the "situation" of such patients, for this is almost unimaginably remote from anything he himself has ever known.

3. Is this a new problem? I've never heard of it before.

Anosognosia in individuals with psychiatric disorders has been known for hundreds of years. Among neurologists, unawareness of illness is well known, since it also occurs in some individuals who have had strokes, brain tumors, Alzheimer's disease, and Huntington's disease. However, in psychiatry, impaired awareness of illness has only become widely discussed since the late 1980s.

4. Is impaired awareness of illness the same thing as denial of illness?

No. Denial is a psychological mechanism which we all use, more or less. Impaired awareness of illness, on the other hand, has a biological basis and is caused by damage to the brain, especially the right hemisphere. The specific brain areas which appear to be most involved are the frontal lobe and part of the parietal lobe.

5. Can a person be partially aware of their illness?

Yes. Impaired awareness of illness is a relative problem, not an absolute one. Some individuals may also fluctuate over time in their awareness, being more aware when they are in remission but losing the awareness when they relapse.

6. Are there ways to improve a person's awareness of their illness?

Studies suggest that approximately one-third of individuals with schizophrenia improve in awareness of their illness when they take antipsychotic medication. Studies also suggest that a larger percentage of individuals with bipolar disorder improve on medication.

7. Why is impaired awareness of illness important in schizophrenia and bipolar disorder?

Impaired awareness of illness is the single biggest reason why individuals with schizophrenia and bipolar disorder do not take medication. They do not believe they are sick, so why should they take medications? Without medication, the person's symptoms become worse. This often makes them more vulnerable to being victimized by others or committing suicide. It also often leads to rehospitalization, homelessness, being incarcerated, and violent acts against others.[98]

8. What are five ways to fully treat those with a clinical depression?

a. Have a complete medical examination to rule out other causes of clinical depression. Some experts have said that thyroid conditions are extremely common in adults from the United States and can often lead to depression—both an overactive thyroid and an underactive one. A simple blood test can diagnose hypothyroidism or hyperthyroidism and lead to appropriate treatment that may be very helpful for relieving depression.

b. Realize that there are certain diseases that can cause depression. Examples of these include a stroke, brain tumor or multiple sclerosis. Degenerative brain diseases, such as Alzheimer's, dementia, Parkinson's disease, or Huntington's disease also frequently cause depression, as does traumatic brain injury. Cardiac conditions are often associated with depression, and treatment for the cardiac condition and depression should begin aggressively at the same time. Psychiatrists need to be thinking as medical doctors when they approach patients who are complaining of depression. At times they may need to order a variety of blood tests, brain images, or EEGs to rule out seizure disorders. And in many cases, psychiatrists need to collaborate closely with primary care doctors and other medical specialists to clarify the diagnosis, and to find and implement the appropriate treatment.

c. Never settle for having a doctor/psychiatrist tell you, "I don't know what else to do; you are just going to have to live with the symptoms." Top researchers tell us that the goals of today's psychiatrists are to control/arrest all of your depressive symptoms. If you have depressive symptoms, you should always be working on a treatment plan to alleviate them. Research suggests that more than half of treatment non-response can be attributed to either poor treatment adherence to a medication regimen and/or to severe side effects. Before making any changes to a medication regimen, the clinician should first ensure that the patient took the prescribed medication consistently and correctly; that the recommended dose was at least a moderate level; and that the patient took the medication for a sufficient duration, typically considered to be at least eight weeks.

d. Consider the possibility that your depression (or part of it) is a spiritual depression. The causes and cures of spiritual depression are numerous: chastisement, vain regrets, false guilt, not understanding what constitutes the doctrine of justification, demoralization, weariness in well doing, and many more.

e. "The cost is too much": This is one of the most difficult barriers to beating a treatment-resistant depression. First, let me say that the evangelical church must concern itself with this blatant need. The Bible tells us that we are to contribute to the needs of the saints (Rom. 12:13). We are to love our brothers and sisters in Christ and be compassionate toward their suffering (Col. 3:12). We are to bear one another's burdens, and thereby fulfill the law of Christ (Gal. 6:2). The government funds for effective treatment of mental illness are drying up. People will be looking to religious nonprofits to take up the slack. Psychiatrists will need to volunteer time in faith-based clinics; pastors will need to be trained in the dynamics of mental illness and depression. If you can get a job, look for one with insurance benefits. If you are poor, apply for Medicaid or for Medicare if you qualify. Find out who the gatekeeper of public mental health is in your county or state, and tap into the resources they have to offer.

It would be advantageous to get a copy of your county services, which care available through the United Way. There are sliding scale-payment plans for low-income persons. Either you or someone else needs to contact the drug company that makes your medicine, and check their programs to help those who do not have insurance.

9. What are antipsychotic medications?

Antipsychotic medicines are primarily used to manage psychosis. The word "psychosis" is used to describe conditions that affect the mind, and in which there has been some loss of contact with reality, often including delusions (false, fixed beliefs) or auditory and visual hallucinations (hearing or seeing things that are not really there). It can be a symptom of a physical condition such as drug abuse, or a mental disorder such as schizophrenia, bipolar disorder, or very severe depression (also known as "psychotic depression").

10. What is the difference between typical and atypical antipsychotics?

Typical and atypical antipsychotics both work to treat symptoms of schizophrenia and the manic phase of bipolar disorder. Several atypical (newer) antipsychotics have a "broader spectrum" of action than the older (typical) medications, and are used for treating bipolar depression or depression that has not responded to treatment. Once the medicine gets into the muscle, it is slowly released into the patient's body over days, weeks, or months.

11. Why are injectable antipsychotic medications so encouraging in the treatment of mental illness?

The injectable antipsychotics that are now available are longer-lasting medications. This type of injection is very important in the treatment of bipolar psychosis, as well as the psychosis of schizophrenia. People who are psychotic are often resistant to treatment. The key to treating psychosis is the use of medications. This is where the problem is: The psychotic person is often paranoid; he also is delusional. There is also an advantage to the injectable medications for someone who is reluctant to take pills on a regular basis but would not mind getting an injection. Days after the injection, he may begin to be more aware of his diagnosis and agree to take tablets or continue the injections. That's where long-lasting drugs can help.

Depending upon the state in which one lives, one can be petitioned into the hospital if he is a danger to himself, to others, or cannot take care of his own basic needs. Once a person is hospitalized and on a regimen of medications, he will begin to "clear" and be more aware of his illness.

12. What are psychotropic medications?

Psychotropic medications, when taken properly, alter brain chemistry by targeting areas of the brain in order to supplement and correct the malfunctioning neurotransmitters and other problems in brain chemistry.

13. If you know the Lord as your Savior, and you are mentally ill, is it right to take medications that affect your brain?

Yes, the brain is part of the body and can be targeted by different medications that God has made available because of scientific evidence. People take medications that help the heart, the pancreas (diabetes), the kidneys, the liver, and for something as simple as a headache. Antipsychotic drugs, antidepressants, and mood stabilizers all target different areas of the brain that have malfunctioned since the moment Adam fell. Drugs are for diseases.

14. What if treatment doesn't help?

Once you've settled on a therapist and doctor, you need to give therapy and medication a chance to work. Getting better takes time, often several months. Treatment for depression can be hard at first. Opening up to someone about very personal things in your life isn't easy, but most people do get better with treatment.

15. What are antidepressants used for?

Antidepressants are used to prevent or treat depression, and/or to stop the recurrence of depression. Antidepressants are not addictive and are not controlled substances such as medications like Klonopin, Ativan, or Xanax.

16. Are there different types of antidepressants?

There are many types of antidepressants, and new ones continue to be formulated. Because of this, patients have a wide range of treatment opportunities when it comes to lifting their dark moods.

17. What are some of the side effects of antidepressants?

Some antidepressants may cause dizziness, dry mouth, increased appetite or weight gain, sexual dysfunction, or nausea. Some of these side effects diminish as a patient continues to take the prescription. There is a "side effect burst" at the beginning, which decreases as one's body adjusts to the medication. Some antidepressants have more side effects than others. A patient may need to try several different antidepressant medications before finding the one that improves the symptoms, while causing side effects that can be managed.

18. What are SSRIs?

SSRIs are *selective serotonin reuptake inhibitors*, and are the most significant class of antidepressants marketed in recent years. They especially help those who have obsessive compulsive disorder, general anxiety disorder, panic disorder, post-traumatic stress disorder, and social anxiety disorder.

19. Are antidepressants addictive?

They are not addictive. They are medicines that treat depression by improving the way the brain uses certain chemicals that control mood or stress.

20. How long does it take for an antidepressant to work?

Psychiatrists believe it takes ten days to six weeks to feel the full effect of the medication.

21. What do I do during the waiting period?

I know the horror of waiting for depression medications to work. You may or may not be able to go to your job. If you can work, do so. Do not put too many demands on yourself; you are in survival mode. If your depression is too severe, you may wish to get electro-convulsive therapy (ECT).

22. When can I go off my medication?

It used to be that medical doctors worked with you to go off your medications. I tried it once in 1992, my doctor agreed with my decision, and it was one of the most horrible decisions I have ever made. I tried to get back on the same medication but they no longer worked. I then tried another antidepressant, and it took a whole month to ascertain that this one did not work. Finally, I was hospitalized and had ECT. After that experiment, I went back to medications and have stayed on them daily ever since.

23. What do you say to people who say that medicine does not get to the root of the problem?

The problem is that when Adam sinned, all of creation was cursed; everything was sentenced to die. Diseases came on the whole earth and continue to do so. The "root of the problem" idea smacks of Freudianism; Freud said something deep within one's psyche needed to be brought up and dealt with in both single free association and through groups of people who had the same type of mental illness. Much of this illogical teaching dominated the United States for at least seventy years and turned mental illness into a neurosis where the disease model had no place.

24. How do I know if I am becoming biologically depressed?

One way to ascertain whether or not it is a biological problem is to monitor your vegetative functions. If you are depressed, biologically, you will normally have severe sleep disturbances, either too much or too little sleep each night. Another vegetative function is the sex drive. Endogenous depressions usually include a low libido or an inability to fully participate in sex. The third vegetative function is the appetite. One in a depressive episode will either overeat or have no appetite at all.

25. Should I work when I am depressed?

If you are able, you should work. As a counselor, there were days when I was more depressed than my clients. It was a testimony, though, the way God would intercede with my workload; a patient would not come for his scheduled appointment and I could get some rest during the day. I worked daily with a moderate depression for years in the 1980s and 1990s.

26. Why do doctors prescribe more than one medicine?

In the 1980s and 1990s, doctors would only prescribe one medicine at a time and wait for six weeks to see if it would lift the mood. I had just about resigned myself to never feeling completely well until the medical profession began to add antidepressants to antidepressants in what they call a "cocktail" to achieve remission of the depression. Because of my rapid downward cycle, a psychiatrist diagnosed me with bipolar II disorder, and added a mood stabilizer to my medications. That was what brought me complete relief.

27. How can I explain my feelings of depression to my loved ones?

Unless a person has experienced a mental illness, it is very difficult to explain how you are feeling. To say you feel sad probably nowhere near describes your psychic pain. By "experiencing mental illness," I don't even mean that someone has to have it, but if they truly love someone who has episodes of depression or any other mental illness, over time, they will start to see the pain and the struggle their loved one feels and their attempts to be well again. I would say, be as patient with them as possible; and then if needs be, tell him or her that you just really need to be alone (or take a walk), whatever seems to be the most helpful at the time. And ask them for patience until you get well again.

28. What kind of expert do I need to see?

People with depression often see a few different experts. You might see a non-MD therapist as well as a doctor or nurse for medicine. The Mental Health Parity and Addiction Equity Act of 2008 requires that health insurance plans do not put restrictions on coverage for mental health services that are different from coverage for other medical or surgical treatment. The Patient Protection and Affordable Care Act provide federal support for low-income individuals to obtain health insurance. Some mental health professionals or clinics also offer a sliding scale based on income.

29. Why can't I just see one doctor?

Your primary care doctor can prescribe antidepressants, but family doctors usually don't have expertise in prescribing drugs for treating psychiatric conditions. So if the first or second antidepressant you try does not help, your doctor may recommend that you see a psychiatrist, who can better prescribe the medicines you need.

30. How do I find a therapist or a psychiatrist?

Ask your regular doctor for a recommendation. You can also get in touch with organizations such as the National Alliance for the Mentally Ill (NAMI), which can suggest experts in your area. Keep in mind that anyone can call himself or herself a therapist. Your therapist should be a licensed psychiatrist, psychologist, social worker, psychiatric nurse, or counselor.

31. What should I look for in a therapist?

Therapists use many different approaches. Some focus on practical, here-and-now issues. Others go deeper, probing events from your past that might have played a role in your depression. There are specific forms of psycho-therapy that have been shown to be helpful for depression, such as cognitive behavior therapy or interpersonal psychotherapy. Many therapists use a mix of styles.

When you first talk to a potential therapist or psychiatrist, ask about his or her approach to see whether it seems appropriate for you and your condition. If it's not a good fit, find someone else. If you don't click with a person, therapy is less likely to be helpful. You may also want to look for someone who specializes in your particular problem. For instance, if you have a problem with drugs or alcohol, find a doctor or nonmedical therapist who specializes in treating people struggling with addiction.

32. What if treatment doesn't help?

Once you've settled on a therapist and doctor, you need to give therapy and medication a chance to work. Getting better takes time, often several months. Treatment for depression can be hard at first. Opening up to someone about very personal things in your life isn't easy. But most people do get better with treatment.

33. What is a generic drug?

A patented medicine eventually becomes open to all manufacturers when the exclusive rights have expired. This is when the generic equivalents become available. It is wise to monitor how you react to each medication and then request the one you find the most helpful from the pharmacy. Or in the USA, you can request a prior authorization for a brand-name drug.

34. Can the symptoms of stress be confused with mental illness?

Scripture speaks about trials and tribulation in life, which are universal to all of us and useful to growth. That translates to stress in today's world. I do not believe that pressure in itself causes mental illness. When mental illness is present, though, stress brings it out into the open because a person's natural resources for dealing with stress are suddenly unavailable.

35. What should I do if the medication that I am taking for my illness is not working, or if it seems to stop working for me?

Many times, a drug will work for you for several years, and then it just seems to stop. At some point, you know that you have to find another drug. It is a common and justified fear for people with psychiatric disorders. Tell your psychiatrist how you feel and that you are not as well as you once were. Ask to try another medication or to explore your diagnosis further. In my case, when I was correctly diagnosed as bipolar II, I was given a mood stabilizer which greatly improved my mental health.

36. My son has bipolar and it is so hard to get him on the right track for treatment. Do you have any advice?

When mental-health professionals assess a person for bipolar disorder, they gather a detailed history and conduct a mental-status examination. The history will explore the possibility that the person's symptoms are caused by a medical condition such as a neurological or endocrine problem, medication side effect, or exposure to a toxin. The profession will also seek to distinguish symptoms of bipolar disorder from other mental-health problems, such as a substance-use disorder, depression, anxiety, or schizophrenia.

Having bipolar disorder can increase the likelihood of the sufferer developing a substance-abuse problem, by potentially more than fifty percent. Some people with bipolar disorder may drink to numb their manic or depressive symptoms, a behavior often referred to as self-medicating. If this is a problem, he needs to see a therapist who knows about both psychotropic medications and substance abuse problems.

Medications are an important and effective part of treating bipolar disorder; these include mood stabilizers, antipsychotics, and anti-seizure medications. All these medications have been found to help even out and prevent the mood swings suffered by individuals with bipolar disorder. Antidepressant medication may trigger mood swings in people with this disorder.

As is the case with other mental disorders, good self-care is an essential part of getting optimal results from talk therapy and medications. People with bipolar disorder should work on getting at least eight hours of sleep per night, exercising regularly, maintaining good nutrition, and avoiding alcohol or drug abuse. When someone has bipolar disorder, she must learn the warning signs for the onset of a manic or depressive episode. That could possibly help them prevent full-blown mood swings.

37. Psychiatrist, psychologist . . . what's the difference?

A psychiatrist is a medical doctor with an additional specialty in psychiatry. He is able to prescribe medications that treat mental illness.

A psychologist is a person who has been educated in studying human behavior and specializes in counseling.

Psychiatrists are very important in the treatment of mental illness. However, most do not practice therapy anymore—mostly, because insurance companies will accept billing for no more than fifteen to thirty minutes (except for the initial diagnostic work-up and crisis intervention).

Another part of this revolution in treatment was the book, *Mood Swings: The Third Revolution in Psychiatry* by Dr. Ronald Fieve.[99] Dr. Peter D. Kramer, who was a medical doctor (trained as a psychiatrist) tells his readers in his book *Listening to Prozac* how medications gave way to therapy in his practice. He was ridiculed by many Freudian therapists and neo-Freudians, who minimizes the biological nature of mental illness. His patients also chided him for doing more therapeutic interventions and fewer biological ones.[100]

The number of psychiatrists is decreasing in the United States. In my practice, I do the assessment and therapy and then go directly to the psychiatrist. This saves horrifying suffering, since the primary mental illness needs medications and needs them as quickly as possible.

Please note that we do not minimize the importance of counseling. I have been a counselor/therapist for many years. My counseling is biblical but I also am a clinically trained pastoral counselor. My master's education included multiple classes as a master of social work.

When a person is mentally ill, he or she needs counseling that helps them understand their mental illness. The biblical counselor must "rightly divide the word of truth." Mental illness needs supportive counseling which explains to them that God views the illness as a trial, suffering from a mental illness will open doors for them to help others.

Practicing psychologists are also trained to administer and interpret a number of tests and assessments that can help diagnose a condition or tell more about the way a person thinks, feels, and behaves. These tests may evaluate intellectual skills, cognitive strengths and weaknesses, vocational aptitude and preference, personality characteristics, and neuropsychological functioning.

38. Who are nouthetic counselors (biblical counselors)?

The Association of Certified Biblical Counselors, or ACBC (formerly known as The National Association of Nouthetic Counselors) has maintained a rigid stance that Christians do not "sign over" counseling to a field they see as founded on atheistic premises. From the onset of the movement, they have denied the biological nature of mental illness, and show little respect for antidepressants and other drugs for mental illness. Does this argument also suggest that Christians should show the same distain for psychiatry, which mostly deals with the medical treatment of mental illnesses?

In my opinion they argue from an *a priori* position—that is, that the Scriptures are sufficient in every area, including mental illness. When I was first biologically depressed, I attended a conference for the General Association of Regular Baptist Churches in Grand Rapids, Michigan. I saw a booth labeled Nouthetic Counselors. I had heard about them, and it just so happened that the head of that organization was in the booth. I told him that I had a clinical depression and knew it was biological. He dismissed my situation with the words, "I won't believe in biological depression until it is proven in a laboratory." This has been the mantra of the ACBC.

As in any movement, the association has made changes. One of them is that they will never advise someone to stop taking antidepressants. There is, of course, a good reason why they would say this: "fear of litigation." I remember when John MacArthur and his church were hit with a lawsuit because one of their converts to Christ had committed suicide after he had stopped taking his antidepressants. Whether or not this young man was advised to do so, I do not know. The case went all the way to the Supreme Court and the parents of the man lost. I am thankful for the court's decision because it validated the separation of church and state. But I can say that Dr. MacArthur has actually said in print that he has advised persons to go off their antidepressant medications.

In his book *Our Sufficiency in Christ*, MacArthur quotes a portion of a letter from a woman who had heard his preaching on the radio. She was diagnosed with bipolar disorder years before this and had taken prescribed medications that helped her with her deep depression and brought her up from thoughts of suicide. She goes on to explain how God had worked in her life. She felt led three years before to stop taking her medication. "Obedience is the key." He applauds her decision. "I believe that testimony. I believe in the power of God's Word. And I grieve that so many seeking people are diverted into humanistic psychology and psychiatry, which only compounds their problems by moving them the wrong direction—away from the sufficiency of Christ and the power of His Word."[101]

Along those lines, an ACBC counselor would never refer a person to a psychiatrist. That would be, in their collective opinion, a step into the secular world of secular sorcery or, humanism, at least. Psychiatrists prescribe medications that make up for the faulty brain chemistry of some people and do not involve themselves with psychoanalysis. They are medical doctors who treat medical diseases.

39. What skepticism does someone with mental illness face from other Christians?

It is unfortunate that a blood-bought child of the King would face skepticism about the treatment of his or her mental illness. Your church friends may give you the cold shoulder. The pastor may make mistakes about mental illness, such as calling someone schizophrenic because they think the functional definition is "split personality."

The church may not support any mentioning of programs for mental illness. If you are a pastor or missionary who has a mental illness, and you are seeking a pastorate, you may be not be asked to candidate for the position. If you become depressed, the deacons of the church may ask you to step down.

Christians may challenge you about using medications. But there are some Christians who will understand your illness, love you, and help you in any way they can. It is important to look at Jesus Christ who is the head of the church and to realize that in the garden of Gethsemane, He was horribly depressed—but continued on to accomplish our redemption by shedding His own blood and enduring the wrath of God on the cross. He now intercedes for all Christians, and that includes those who have bipolar disorder, schizophrenia, and other sicknesses of the mind and mood.

40. What support is recommended for a caregiver/family?

Caregivers and family members need encouragement as they assist the one who is suffering. Mental illness is a family disease, and if possible caregivers should find a support group. There are support groups available for the secular world and those can be beneficial. Part of our CAMI (Christians Afflicted with Mental Illness) ministry is a support group ministry. The groups are made up of those who have the illnesses, as well as their family members, parents, and friends who want to learn how to be a help and find courage to continue assisting the people they love. Support would also be useful in other settings such as small groups (fellowship), adult Bible studies, recovery groups, and the like.

41. Sometimes I think that God doesn't love me, because He allowed me to have a mental illness.

You cannot understand the true meaning of suffering unless you understand who God really is and what He has in store for His redeemed people. I have learned, through the school of suffering and by reading God's Word, some very important things.

First, God is not obligated to give an all-inclusive answer to us as to our suffering. He does not owe me an explanation for His dealings, even when they involve me. He is the Potter; He can do with His clay as He wishes.

Second, suffering reveals what is in our hearts and gives us the opportunity to trust God. Suffering is the fire that heats the gold and separates it from the imperfections.

> In this you greatly rejoice, even though now for a little while, if necessary, you have been distressed by various trials, so that the proof of your faith, being more precious than gold which is perishable, even though tested by fire, may be found to result in praise and glory and honor at the revelation of Jesus Christ (1 Peter 1:6–7).

Third, God is my Father—the Father of mercy and God of all comfort. Whenever there is suffering in the life of a Christian, comfort overflows (see 2 Cor. 1:4). Sometimes the comfort is delayed, but God's comfort is always greater than our suffering. We read in James 5:11:

> We count those blessed who endured. You have heard of the endurance of Job and have seen the outcome of the Lord's dealings that the Lord is full of compassion and is merciful.

Perhaps you are in the middle of intense suffering. The jury may be out, but when the trial is over, if you have endured, you will discover for yourself that the Lord is "full of compassion and merciful."

> Be still my soul! The Lord is on thy side; Bear patiently the cross of grief or pain; Leave to thy God to order and provide; in every change He faithful will remain. Be still my soul! Thy best, thy heavenly friend, Thro' thorny ways leads to a joyful end.[102]

Fourth, suffering is a privilege that God entrusts to His children. Philippians 1:29–30 says:

> For to you it has been granted for Christ's sake, not only to believe in Him, but also to suffer for His sake, experiencing the same conflict which you saw in me, and now hear to be in me.

As the Puritan Thomas Goodwin said, "God's champions are often in the dark." He entrusts some of His choicest people to suffer intensely. North American Christians especially need to hear about the gift of suffering. We look at the Scriptures through the lens of our ethical hedonistic culture, which values the absence of pain and suffering as an ideal. In reality, the believer's suffering is a blessing.

Fifth, suffering is wisely appointed by God and fitted for us. Such was the case when Peter was told that he would one day be killed on a cross. He immediately asked whether John also would face execution. Jesus said, "What is that to *you*? *You* follow me!" (John 21:22, emphasis added).

42. Can you be sick (mentally ill) and still be in the will of God?

I have been sick a number of times in my life. I had kidney stones in my early twenties. I became very sick at age twenty-nine with what was a clinical depression, and it affected my whole body. I could not sleep, nor eat, and I had no sex drive. My family had to go on food stamps and Medicaid and we had to move into the basement of our relatives. Even now, I am on medication which has arrested the illness but not cured it. Mental illness, for me, has meant many episodes of depression.

I remember many years ago, when I was working for an aluminum company. I had a cold and one of my coworkers, who was a Christian, encouraged me to "rebuke the demon" that was causing my cold. What a trite nonbiblical approach to sickness! If I believed in a health, wealth, and prosperity gospel, I would have given up long ago. Even Paul the apostle said about one of his powerful missionaries, "Trophimus I left sick at Miletus" (2 Tim. 4:20).

In fact, Paul himself had a terrible disease, which he called a "thorn in the flesh." He asked God three times to take it from him—he even had the gift of healing—but the Lord's answer was to him was that He would not take it away. Why not? According to Paul:

> Because of the surpassing greatness of the revelations, for this reason, to keep me from exalting myself, there was given me a thorn in the flesh, a messenger of Satan to torment me—to keep me from exalting myself (2 Cor. 12:7).

43. As a caregiver, I sometimes think, "Why don't you just pull yourself together and get back to your duties in life? Am I wrong?

(I am letting my wife write the answer to this, as a caregiver).

When Steve was first depressed, I was in the dark about as much as any human being could be. I had never seen anything like whatever it was that had overtaken my fun and self-sacrificing husband. First he had become sick with flu-like symptoms and then horribly, *horribly* depressed. He didn't sleep or eat, he couldn't make any decisions, and he didn't want me to leave his side. I remember looking at him and saying, "I could whip you right now, couldn't I?" He just nodded his head. He was so sad! We were a happy couple, married six years, and had three beautiful children, ages five, three and our newborn baby boy! What was there to be sad about? Then to top off our supposedly joyous time, we were offered our first church for Steve to pastor. That bit of good news cheered me right up! It did nothing for Steve.

I had a very long way to go in understanding depression. My only thought was that he had never acted like this; something was very different. As time went on, I started to realize that it had to have a physical cause. He started trying medications and reading in the library to try to learn what it was that had taken over his brain. (His family, by the way, was riddled with depression and bipolar disorder, but except for feeling badly that they were sick, we didn't pay that much attention.)

For almost two years, Steve dragged himself around, studying for his graduate degree and working two jobs, still at least moderately depressed. I could see that he had ups and downs, and that some medications were better than others. Finally, he asked a doctor to try one more medication and by the end of one week, he seemed more talkative. By the end of the second week, he was better! He was back!

I saw him pray from a prayer list because his concentration was bad, and he started carrying an index card with a few Bible verses on it in his shirt pocket since he couldn't really read large parts of the Bible as he always had. He persevered through a storm I only witnessed from a nearby pavilion. Oh, I saw the clouds and heard the thunder; I felt the wind and had some genuine fear of the torrential rains, but he weathered it. He faced the lightning and the hurricane forces as they hit him head on.

Did I watch him walk out of that tempest and find him weak? Did I ever wish he could have stood with me under the shelter? Oh, yes. Could he have done more while the winds were raging? No. He fought nobly and faithfully and survived!

Sometimes people have said, "Don't you think depressed people are self-centered? All they ever talk about is their depression." My answer is that I have had four children and that when I was in the pain of labor, I didn't really care if the nurse was having a good day or how the doctor would be spending her afternoon. I wanted somebody to do something and help me get this baby out of my body and into the world! I wasn't being selfish. I was in pain.

When Steve was depressed, yes, he talked about his depression, he was quiet and struggling. Sometimes he paced and cried. Was he selfish? *No*. He was in pain. He is the bravest person I know, because he survived. He didn't take his own life. He didn't leave me alone with our children. He persevered, and every other time he has gotten depressed, I have told him, "I will wait until you come back. And I know you will. The meds will work and you will be fine again."

So, I would say that if you, as a caregiver, can assure your spouse or friend that your lives together will be intact when he or she is better, that goes a long way toward encouraging him or her. If it is your son or daughter, the suffering is very difficult to watch. Go with them to the doctor's appointments if they will allow you. You can help establish a good history of the illness for the patient who may be unable to express all that needs to be said. Be sure to encourage her that she will be well again and that you will do whatever it takes to make sure of it.

Those who survive these episodes of mental illness crises are not weak; they are the strongest people I know. If they can persevere through these storms, they deserve a lot of credit. Give support, help them when they are at their weakest, try not to second-guess the causes of the illness, and assure them you will be there when they are well again. When a person survives the horrors of a mental break, he or she deserves a loving welcome home, not a note or text message that it became too much for the one watching.

Proverbs has a word to say about those who fail to comfort the depressed and brokenhearted. Proverbs 25:20 uses a Hebrew root word that sometimes denotes a Jewish bard or minstrel who would go from place to place telling folktales and singing fun songs: "Like one who takes off a garment on a cold day, or like vinegar on soda, is he who sings songs to a troubled heart."

How easy it is for those who have not felt the dark gloom and bitter pain of depression to tell the depressed or brokenhearted that they can easily overcome it. Such empty advice is cold comfort that makes matters worse for the sufferer.

Does that mean that only those who have experienced depression can understand it well enough to help? A pastor said to me, half in jest, "I haven't been depressed a day in my life . . . and it's not my fault." This pastor recognized that the one who has not experienced a particular sort of crisis will be less prepared to help others deal with it. Those who have not experienced mental illness must take to heart Paul's advice in Romans 12:15, "Rejoice with those who rejoice, weep with those who weep." To show Christ's love, it is sometimes needful simply to weep with those who are weeping, rather than give superficial advice or try to be cheery. Job's friends were good comforters as long as they sat in silence. It was when they opened their mouths to preach long, superficial sermons that they were used of Satan to drive Job into deeper despair.

44. What are some things I need to know about secular psychiatry?

I would like to look at some of the basic underlying assumptions that are part of a secular psychiatry which includes a bias against the supernatural, whether it is God or Satan. We do cover the difference between demon-possession and schizophrenia in our seminars, though here we discuss the subject with brevity.

My assumption is that as a culture gets further and further away from God, more people in that culture will practice witchcraft and there will be more occurrences of demon-possession. But the flip side of this is that a culture that does not honor Scripture will often deny the existence of demons as well as the existence of God. Demonic doctrine is organized, powerful, and deceptive. Paul writes:

> But the Spirit explicitly says that in later times some will fall away from the faith, paying attention to deceitful spirits and doctrines of demons (1 Tim. 4:1).

In the 1970s, the Soviet Union authorities sent evangelical pastors to psychiatric hospitals; psychiatrists prescribed them medications that normally were used for the treatment for bipolar disorder. Those in the Soviet Union did not believe in God or in anything that was supernatural. This deluded thinking was a result of the deceptive doctrine of demons mentioned above.

I have also read and pieced together that this bias against the supernatural, and more specifically against the work of the Holy Spirit in revival and conversion, was part of the psychiatric treatment practiced by the mad doctors of the eighteenth-century England. These English psychiatrists actually petitioned the court to hospitalize the despised Wesleyans because they had ecstatic utterances. Some of these evangelicals were put in the infamous Bedlam Hospital.

I remember the desperation I felt when I was looking for a psychiatrist who would prescribe the medicine I needed to alleviate the symptoms of my clinical depression. I found a doctor in a neighboring town who was no help to me; he ridiculed me because he felt that evangelical Christians should have "the joy of the Lord." He also told me that John the Baptist suffered from psychosis and depression. Since part of psychosis is hearing voices, I assume the "psychosis" to which this doctor referred is found in Matthew:

> After being baptized, Jesus came up immediately from the water; and behold, the heavens were opened, and he saw the Spirit of God descending as a dove *and* lighting on Him, and behold, a voice out of the heavens said, "This is]My beloved Son, in whom I am well-pleased" (Matt. 3:16–17).

45. Do you think that the devil is using my mental illness to defeat me?

Any time you feel like giving up the Christian life—or are so discouraged, in so much despair that you feel swallowed up by doubts, depression, and fear—you can bet the devil is using your mental illness to defeat you.

You need the armor of God. Now obviously, an extensive study of the subject of spiritual warfare and the armor of God would take too much space, so I will say a few words about the "devil wanting to eat you for dinner." What I mean is, Satan wants to overwhelm you with sorrow. This is one of his foremost goals. Since the beginning of time, he has been devouring those who have believed in God and Messiah, Jesus. Satan and his demons are very active throughout today's world. This passage demonstrates this activity:

> Finally, be strong in the Lord and in the strength of His might. Put on the full armor of God, so that you will be able to stand firm against the schemes of the

devil. For our struggle is not against flesh and blood, but against the rulers, against the powers, against the world forces of this darkness, against the spiritual forces of wickedness in the heavenly places (Eph. 6:10–12).

The Greek word for schemes in the Ephesians passage is *methodia*. He uses methods which involve cunning arts, deceit, craft, and trickery. Satan is a highly intelligent being and actually, is a commander. He and his army (demons) formulate many different strategies to cause God's people to sin. And his fighting is up close and personal. He wants you to be swallowed up by fear and panic, so that you will give up living the Christian life the way it should be lived. You have to put on the full armor of God. You must read your Bible prayerfully. You must take up the shield of faith. If you are not aware of his schemes, then he has already defeated you.

46. How can parents recognize that their children have a mental health disorder?

The most important thing is that parents have to know their kids. They have to recognize what their appetites, sleep patterns, social activities, and academic performances are like. When there are changes in those behaviors, that should be a red flag. It's important to consider that there is a general discrepancy between a parent's and child's report on the degree and nature of the illness. Children report more illness about themselves than their parents report about them, particularly if they are anxious or depressed. Parents don't see the symptoms as often as the child does. That means if a parent sees a change, they shouldn't wait. It's most likely more severe than they suspect. Children do not naturally talk about how worried, sad, or irritable they are.

47. What happens when a child with mental illness is not treated?

I think the worst thing that that can happen to a child is they can have damage to their self-esteem. They start feeling "less than" or inadequate. That happens if they are put in situations where they don't have the skills to succeed or to thrive. If we pretend that a child doesn't have a problem, and yet they can't sit still or pay attention as long as other kids, or they can't pick up the language the way everyone else can, or they're so anxious that they can't concentrate, we put children into a real-life situation on a daily basis where they are feeling truly inadequate. They become demoralized. They want to avoid that situation.

That, in my opinion, is what contributes to the high rate of academic failure and school dropout that occurs with kids who have a psychiatric diagnosis. Seventy percent of the youth in juvenile justice settings have a psychiatric diagnosis. When left untreated, kids start feeling bad, and when someone feels bad in a situation they try to avoid it. Once you start avoiding school, you are more at risk for bad things happening to you.

48. What would you say to parents who may be reluctant to put their child on medication?

These medications are specific and they target the brain. If your child is suffering greatly and there is medicine that works, you may be compelled to use medication. It is important that a psychiatrist do this, and often a child psychiatrist in conjunction with a pediatrician. Some type of therapy is also important for both children and parents.

49. What else should parents know about mental health treatment?

Sometimes a child will need more than just therapy and one medicine. You might need two medicines. Some of these are hard conditions to treat. Parents who are concerned about using medication need to have an understanding of how medicine works. Medicine seems to give a quicker response, and gets your kid less symptomatic, faster. But by no stretch of the imagination is medicine a magic bullet. Cognitive behavioral therapy can really make a world of difference in the long run for these kids.

50. Finding help for a child can be difficult, time-consuming and expensive, as many providers do not take insurance. What can be done to make this easier for parents?

Parents are so worried and distressed when they finally decide to get mental health care for their kids that they don't do the due-diligence process that we think is necessary. There is a symptom checker on the website of Child Mind Institute (www.childmind.org/symptomchecker) that gives some idea of what may be troubling their child. This is where parents really need help. They need to understand when their child is in trouble, and they have to make sure they are getting their kids truly effective treatment.

Parents have a hard job. Part of the requirement of being a good parent is to not to deny when you see symptoms. In the hopes that you want your kids to be healthy, sometimes we tend to look the other way. But this is really one of those times when looking the other way can be detrimental to the child.

51. What is the difference between ADHD and bipolar disorder?

While ADHD is chronic or ongoing, bipolar disorder is usually episodic, with periods of normal mood interspersed with depression, mania, or hypomania. A diagnosis of ADHD versus bipolar disorder requires a lot of history to be taken—or as a psychiatrist once told me when I asked how to distinguish between the two, "history, history, and more history."

52. Why do pastors latch on to verses in the New Testament about the subject of anxiety, but don't use the Psalms or the wonderful Isaiah passages that speak about the love of God and grace extended to His people?

I, too, have personally felt guilty after hearing those sermons. Peter speaks about anxiety and how we should cast it on the Lord. If you have an anxiety disorder, this will be more difficult. You must remember this is a command of love, not of the law. You do the best you can; God expects no more. Peter's incentive for the command is found after the command itself, "casting all your anxiety on Him, because He cares for you" (1 Peter 5:7).

Another part of my explanation is that there is a failure on the part of pastors and Christian counselors to understand "the parsimony principle." I first read about this years ago in a book called the *Greatness of the Kingdom* by Alva McClain. He was answering a complaint that people were raising, as to why is there not more about the millennial kingdom in the book of Revelation. McClain states:

> Of course, if such an argument has any validity at all, it could be brought against the doctrines of any sort of a kingdom whether spiritual or otherwise. But all such arguments ignore what has been called the principle of "parsimony" in Scripture. The Old Testament prophets had described this future Mediatorial Kingdom in great detail and for those acquainted with the Old Testament there would be no need for any profuse repetition of what was already revealed.[103]

He goes on to say that Christ modeled the parsimony principle for us:

> If men went wrong in their ideas of the Kingdom, He pointed to the source of their error: "You do err, not knowing the Scriptures" (Matthew 22:29). And the Scriptures here, it is sometimes forgotten, are those of the Old Testament.[104]

Many pastors, especially those who wish to criticize people about being anxious, use these Scriptures as proof texts to support their pastoral theology. We should read through the Old Testament every year. When we counsel others, we should use the wisdom literature of the Old Testament as well as the New Testament.

53. I just have depression. Why do people have to call depression mental illness?

Depression is called the "common cold" of mental illness. "Depression" is a word which is understood many ways in the English language. If you mean by having depression that you feel "down" for a little while because you didn't get an A on a test, or because your boyfriend broke up with you, that

8

is different from clinical depression. One writer called depression a "brain storm," which is really closer to how a person feels with a clinical depression. It affects more than mood; it interferes with you socially, vocationally, and with your vegetative functioning.

54. What if a Christian commits suicide? Will he go to hell?

If you are a true believer in Christ and His finished work on the cross, you will not go to hell. Suicide is a sin, but, the moment a person is saved, his sins, past, present and future are all forgiven. He is eternally secure (John 10:27–30), he is justified, and his ultimate redemption is the saving of his body and soul, or "glorification" (Rom. 5:1–2). If a Christian man is committing adultery and dies during the act, he will go to heaven even if he did not have time to confess and repent of his sin. If you are counseling a depressed Christian who is suicidal, you should point out that suicide is self-murder and will have terrible consequences on earth and may include a "loss of rewards" at the bema seat of Christ.

55. What is the difference between a reactive depression and a biological depression?

The term "reactive depression" is not used nearly as much as it was twenty to forty years ago. A person may feel depressed as a grief reaction to a life event or loss. It is unlike endogenous depression, which is caused by faulty brain chemistry. Endogenous depression has unrelenting sorrow, loss of hope, depression, constant sleep disturbance, loss of appetite, and often loss of sex drive.

Reactive depressions (also called exogenous depressions) are very distressing and often occur during holidays and anniversaries. It involves a person reacting to a life event. They come from outward circumstances, feelings of loss, and inadequate coping resources. Reactive depressions can include a response to particular life pressures and, of course, a reaction to loss of a cherished object or dream. For example, a person wants Christmas to be the way it used to be before the death of a loved one. Now they sit at the holiday table and there is an empty chair, causing deep pain. The missed loved one's absence—in this case, permanent absence—engenders a reaction of grief and loss.

Reactive depressions may also be a result of someone who has been devastated by an unwanted divorce; they begin to think "if only it could be like it was when we were first married; we were so happy." The loss of the past and the future haunts them daily. But there is a certain resilience in the reactively depressed person's mood, especially as time goes on.

Sometimes parents torture themselves with thoughts of what it would be like if their children were godly and cry out like David, over the prodigal, "O Absalom, my son, my son." Reactive depression should not be suppressed or suffocated. It is something that is very real and it needs to "run its course."

Reactive depression can also be spiritual in nature. Job, who had lost all of his children and everything he possessed, laments:

> Oh, that I were as in months gone by, as in the days when God watched over me; when His lamp shone over my head, and by His light I walked through darkness; as I was in the prime of my days, when the friendship of God was over my tent; when the Almighty was yet with me, and my children were around me; when my steps were bathed in butter, and the rock poured out for me streams of oil (Job 29:2–6).

Understanding God and His purposes are important in resolving this kind of depression. Job was boxed in by his sorrows, and only God Himself could bring him through, out of the deep waters and the sorrowful pit from which he could not climb. A lowering of expectations can be helpful; being thankful for who you are and what you have in Christ is a wonderful way to look at life. Recognizing God's sovereign purpose in trials is an overriding theme in Scripture. Peter, in his first epistle, after he spoke to his readers about their eternal inheritance and salvation tells them:

> In this you greatly rejoice, even though now for a little while, if necessary, you have been distressed by various trials (1 Peter 1:6).

The "little while" is life—the dash on a grave stone—in comparison with eternal glory. The distress is only for a little while compared to eternity. God has deemed it something that is needed during our stay on earth.

56. How do you distinguish grief from a major depressive episode?

In distinguishing grief from a major depressive episode (MDE), it is useful to consider that in grief the predominant effect is feelings of emptiness and loss, while in MDE it is a persistent depressed mood and the inability to anticipate happiness or pleasure.

The dysphoria in grief is likely to decrease in intensity over days to weeks and occurs in waves—the so-called pangs of grief. These waves tend to be associated with thoughts or reminders of the deceased. The depressed mood of a MDE is more persistent and is not tied to thoughts or preoccupations. The pain of grief may be accompanied by positive emotions and humor that are uncharacteristic of the pervasive unhappiness and misery characteristic of a major depressive episode. The thought content associated with grief generally features a preoccupation with thoughts and memories of the deceased, rather than the self-critical or pessimistic ruminations seen in MDE.

In grief, self-esteem is generally preserved; whereas in a MDE, feelings of worthlessness and loathing are common. If self-derogatory ideation is present in grief, it typically involves perceived failings vis-à-vis the deceased. (i.e., not visiting frequently enough, not telling the deceased how much he or she was loved). If a bereaved individual thinks about death and dying, such thoughts are generally focused on the deceased and possibly about "joining" the deceased; whereas in a major depressive episode such thoughts are focused on ending one's own life because of feeling worthless, undeserving of life, or unable to cope with the pain of depression.

57. What does it mean that depression is a neurodegenerative disease?

As a leading expert in biological psychiatry research puts it, "So it's [depression] not as benign an illness as we used to suppose. It tends to be recurrent, it tends to run down hill; and so one should, in the face of several episodes, consider long-term preventative treatment to avoid all horrible consequences. This suggests that depression, even if it is occasioned by external tragedy, ultimately changes the structure, as well as the biochemistry of the brain."[105]

58. What do you think of weaning off my medications?

Frequently patients who are responsive to their medications decide to "wean" themselves off of their medication, supposing this to be an end goal. When they start to have symptoms return and decide to restart the same medication, it sometimes doesn't help anymore. Cycling on and off medications is not advisable. There is an increased risk that the depression will become chronic and inescapable.

Since treatment by medication is the most effective treatment for depression and mental illness (schizophrenia, bipolar disorder, etc.) and since not taking these medications (antidepressants, antipsychotics, mood stabilizers), or stopping them, often results in altering the chemistry of the brain, the question is: Why would you object to a person taking medication? Another question is: Why would you discourage a person from getting help by taking these medications, since they are not addictive or harmful to the brain but beneficial?

This is the reason we oppose our Christian brothers who counsel their clients to stop taking their medications. It is looked upon as a weakness to remain on psychotropic drugs and the result is painful mental illness, permanent brain damage, and guilt for having to take medications in the first place. At Heartfelt Counseling Ministries we do biblical counseling, link clients to good psychiatric care, support them through their episodes, and teach them about their illnesses.

APPENDIX A: DIAGNOSTIC DIFFERENTIALS

The determination by which one of two or more diseases or conditions a patient is suffering from, by systematically comparing and contrasting their clinical findings (*Dorland's Illustrated Medical Dictionary*, Elsevier, 2003).

Demoralization: To deprive a person or persons of spirit, courage, discipline; to destroy the morale of someone or some group of people.	**Clinical Depression:** A biological disease resulting from faulty brain chemistry
Caused by a specific stress or stressors which undermine the confidence or the morale of a person	May be triggered by stress (especially the first episode), but mood will remain depressed unless alleviated by psychiatric intervention
Will yield to effective treatment to improve one's condition and remove the stressor which is causing demoralization.	Removing stressor doesn't change depressed mood.
Has a certain resilience; good news will cheer up; time can lessen the intensity	Depression is flat-line, either severe or moderate; changing the environment is of little help
Can occur with a person who has a severe, lifetime mental illness. The person may have some relief but successive losses can break the morale, making it difficult to cope with recurring episodes	Due to faulty brain chemistry; when chemistry is off-kilter, one needs a psychiatrist.

Biblical Example of Demoralization (burnout): Jacob	Biblical Example of Depression: Heman, the poet/singer, is a great example of clinical/biological depression:
• Joseph, the son of his old age, was presumed to be killed by wild beasts • His favorite wife Rachel died in childbirth. • Rebecca's nurse died. • Reuben had slept with his father's concubine. • His two sons killed Hamor the Shechemite in a murderous fashion. • Simeon was in prison. • All changed when he heard Joseph was alive, Simeon was safe, and there was a wonderful place for them all to live in Egypt. • The Hebrew word for "revive," *chayah*, means, "to live, have life, remain alive, sustain life, and to be quickened. He said, "It is enough my son Joseph is alive. I will go see him before I die" (Gen. 47:28). • No signs of major depression • He did have reactive depression symptoms in all these grief reactions.	• DSM–5 says that one of the criteria for major depression is having a (1) depressed mood (2) loss of interest or pleasure for most of the day, nearly every day, for at least two weeks. • Psalm 88:4, 6: "I am reckoned among those who go down to the pit. . . . You have put me in the lowest pit, In dark places, in the depths." Pit is a metaphor for depression. • DSM–5: Fatigue or loss of energy practically every day • Psalm 88:4b: "I have become like a man without strength." • Psalm 88:16: "Your burning anger has passed over me; Your terrors have destroyed me." The Hebrew word for wrath is *chemah*, which is defined as venom, poison (fig.) burning anger, rage, hot displeasure, indignation, and anger, even sometime fever. • DSM–5: Feelings of guilt inappropriate and constant, also feelings of worthlessness • Psalm 88:16: Guilt, worthlessness—"Your burning anger has passed over me; your terrors have destroyed me." • DSM–5: Insomnia nearly every day • Psalm 88:1: "O LORD, the God of my salvation, I have cried out by day and in the night before You." • DSM–5: Symptoms cause clinically significant distress or impairment in social, occupational or other important areas of functioning • Psalm 88:8: "You have removed lover and friend far from me; my acquaintances are in darkness."

In Acts 26:24, Paul is accused by Festus of being manic: "Festus said in a loud voice, 'Paul, you are out of your mind! Your great learning is driving you mad.'"

Paul "normal brain"	Festus Accuses Paul of Mania
Paul gave his testimony (Acts 26:13–19) that he had a vision of Jesus who told him to stop persecuting Him and his people. He also spoke of the resurrection of the dead and affirmed that he believed it. "So, King Agrippa, I did not prove disobedient to the heavenly vision."	"Paul, you are out of your mind! Your great learning is driving you mad." Festus thought that only madmen had visual and auditory hallucinations.
Acts 26:25: But Paul said, 'I am not out of my mind, most excellent Festus, but I utter words of sober truth.'" The word for "sober" can be translated "a sound mind." Acts 26:8: "Why is it considered incredible among you people if God does raise the dead?"	It is apparent from the context that Festus did not believe in the resurrection, though if Festus were honest about the truth, he would have believed in Christ.
Paul did not back down but preached the gospel. This presentation always included the death, burial, and resurrection of Jesus Christ.	Festus, no doubt, believed that Paul was insane. Paul therefore appealed to King Agrippa, whom Festus had invited to the trial.
	This principle that unbelievers concluded that prophets who saw visions and heard voices were insane is throughout Scripture. For instance, 2 Kings 9:11; Hosea 9:7; John 10:20; Acts 12:15; 1 Corinthians 14:23.

Spiritual Depression	Biological Depression
Misunderstanding God's providence in our lives	By its nature, clinical depression produces negative thoughts and guilt.
Chastening, if not responded to correctly, will bring depression (Heb. 12:5).	Biological depression in bipolar disorder will shift from mania to depression. It is not affected by a stimulus other than poor brain chemistry.
Trials	
Being swallowed up by one of Satan's devices, i.e., being deceived into sinning and then being deceived in thinking that we can never be forgiven.	Biological depression can be considered to be a very severe trial. Before the biological revolution in psychiatry there was little hope in stopping or delaying depression. We should use every medical means to alleviate the sufferers of these diseases.
Persecution and the believer's response to it (1 Peter 4:12–19)	Persons who are tortured, or are prisoners, often get PTSD and reactive depression, which can also trigger a biological depression
Lack of faith	
Abstain from fleshly lusts which wage war against your soul (1 Peter 2:11–12).	One cannot fight sin by taking medication. Meditate on Acripture and it will affect your inner man.

Reactive Depression	Biological (Endogenous) Depression
Grief response to a life event or loss	Can come upon a person out of nowhere
Mood has some resiliency and can improve in time	Flatness, and deadness to the mood with no relief
Depression often recurs, esp. on holidays	Not affected by holidays, good or bad
Can be fueled by poor coping mechanisms	Can be impossible to cope, leading to suicide
Over-sleep is possible, as an escape mechanism	Can oversleep or not sleep enough

Schizophrenia	Demon-Possession
Positive symptoms: Delusions, hallucinations (hearing voices, or seeing things that are not real) and disorganized thoughts	Mark 5:15: After Gadarene demoniac has demons cast out and comes to know Christ, he is said to be in his "right mind." Greek here is (*sofroneo*) to be of sound mind, to exercise control.
There is at this point no cure for schizophrenia. The brain's cells are not firing correctly. He has conceptual disorganization. Negative symptoms: Inability to react to surroundings or trouble, very weak	Before having the demons cast out: Reacting violently or with unusual strength, speaking in a different voice. He knows the devil is possessing but cannot resist him.
Lack of emotion, loss of eye contact, facial expression flat and slowed speech, not talking He can have some normalcy through medications.	Roaring and screaming, threatening others, no fear, commanding, engaging others
Fearful, withdrawn	He likes to engage others and terrify them by this
Could be out of touch with reality and naked	Naked, but clothed after salvation
Lives in the inner city usually to access services	Dwelling around tombs, cutting on himself
Responds, at least to some extent, to antipsychotic medications, not exorcism	Does not respond to antipsychotic medications; responds to salvation through Christ

APPENDIX B:
OVERVIEW OF MEDICATIONS

The importance of dealing with the medical approach to mental illness cannot be overemphasized. Christians are still being advised against taking drugs for depression, bipolar disorder, and other mental disorders because their pastors and other Christian counselors see these illnesses as rooted in sin. The carnage left behind is astounding and heartbreaking. It is a sad truth that many Christian counselors continue to demand more evidence of the biological component to mental illness when it has already been verified medically.

I am a practicing therapist and pastoral counselor, so I understand the value of behavior therapy. The medications are in no way suggestive for prescribing or advising purposes. I feel it is wise enough for pastors to be somewhat familiar with the type of medications and what their primary uses are, as your members and counselees come to you for help. I have found that these medications are so foreign to most pastors that in many cases they may not know where to start. Here is your starting point.

Pastors need to be aware of psychotropic medications and how they function. Psychotropic medications, when taken properly, alter brain chemistry by targeting areas of the brain in order to supplement and correct the malfunctioning neurotransmitters and other problems in brain chemistry. Christians take medications for the heart, pancreas, kidneys, liver—any body part that ails them. Yet when we get anywhere near the brain, they call it spiritual. Why is the brain any different?

The goal of medication is to alleviate the distressing symptoms. Some psychiatric disorders are harder than others to obtain a full remission. In fact, mainstream psychiatrists are beginning to look outside the box when it comes to some of the lingering symptoms of mental illness. Fish oil, antioxidants, and other supplements are being used in the psychiatric world. This is especially true when it comes to major depression. I am compelled to explain to pastors (and others who serve the mentally ill population) the different categories of psychotropic medications and the functions they perform in the brain.

Why should I feel I have to defend the research that helps the mentally ill, when throughout history we have all benefitted from medical science and the brilliant minds that keep us living better and stronger lives? After all, from the creation of male and female, we have been using research and skills to create a better world. The cultural mandate or creation mandate is the divine injunction found in Genesis 1:26, in which God, after having created the world and all in it, ascribes to humankind the tasks of filling, subduing, and ruling over the earth.

Antipsychotic drugs, antidepressants, mood stabilizers, anti-anxiety and ADHD medications all target different areas of the brain that have malfunctioned since Adam fell. As Charles Spurgeon once said, "At the fall of man, everyone lost a shingle off his roof."

ANTIDEPRESSANT MEDICATIONS

Antidepressant medications are medicines that treat depression. They do so by regulating neurotransmitters of the brain, such as serotonin, norepinephrine, and dopamine. In the United States, new antidepressant formulations are approved by the Food and Drug Administration (FDA).

ANTIDEPRESSANT MEDICATIONS			
Brand name	Generic name	Used as	Class
Anafranil	Clomipramine	Antidepressant	Tricyclic, atypical
Celexa	Citalopram	Antidepressant	SSRI
Cymbalta	Duloxetine	Antidepressant	SNRI
Desyrel	Trazadone	Antidepressant	tricyclic
Effexor	Venlafaxine	Antidepressant	SNRI
Effexor XR	Venlafaxine XR	Antidepressant	SNRI
Elavil	amitriptyline	Antidepressant	Tricyclic
Emsam (patch)	selegiline	Antidepressant	MAOI
Fetzima	No generic, until 2023	Antidepressant	SNRI
Lexapro	Escitalopram	Antidepressant	SSRI
Luvox	Fluvoxamine	Antidepressant	SSRI
Nardil	Phenelzine	Antidepressant	MAOI
Norpramine	Desipramine	Antidepressant	Tricyclic
Pamelor	Nortriptyline	Antidepressant	Tricyclic
Parnate	Tranylcypromine	Antidepressant	MAOI
*Paxil	Paroxetine	Antidepressant	SSRI
Pristiq	Desvenlafaxine	Antidepressant	SNRI
Prozac	Fluoxetine	Antidepressant	SSRI
Remeron	Mirtazapine	Antidepressant	Atypical Tetracyclic
Sinequan	Doxepin	Antidepressant	Tricyclic

ANTIDEPRESSANT MEDICATIONS

Brand name	Generic name	Used as	Class
Symbyax	Olanzapine/Fluoxetine	Atypical antidepressant and antipsychotic	SSRI and atypical antipsychotic
Tofranil	Imipramine	Antidepressant	Tricyclic
Trintellix	Vortioxetine	Antidepressant	Serotonin Modulator
Vibryd	Vilazodone	Antidepressant	SSRI Atypical
Wellbutrin LA	Bupropion LA	Antidepressant	Atypical
Wellbutrin SR	Bupropion SR	Antidepressant	Atypical
Zoloft	Sertraline	Antidepressant	SSRI

Fluoxetine (Prozac), Sertraline (Zoloft), Escitalopram (Lexapro), Paroxetine (Paxil), and Citalopram (Celexa) are some of the most commonly prescribed SSRIs for depression. Most are available in generic versions. SSRIs have been shown to be effective in treating not only depression only but also obsessive-compulsive disorder and panic disorder. Serotonin and norepinephrine reuptake inhibitors (SNRIs) block the reabsorption (reuptake) of the neurotransmitters and norepinephrine in the brain.

SSRIs and SNRIs tend to have fewer side effects than older antidepressants, but they sometimes produce headaches, nausea, jitters, or insomnia when people first start to take them. This is known as a burst of symptoms, which tend to fade with time. Some people also experience sexual problems with SSRIs or SNRIs, which may be helped by adjusting the dosage or switching to another medication.

Norepinephrine and dopamine are in another class of reuptake inhibitors, but they are represented by only one drug, Wellbutrin (Bupropion), which tends to have similar side effects as SSRIs and SNRIs, but it is less likely to cause ED (erectile dysfunction). Sometimes stimulants, anti-anxiety medications, or other medications are used together with an antidepressant, especially if a person has a coexisting illness. However, neither anti-anxiety medications nor stimulants are effective against depression when taken alone, and both should be taken only under a doctor's close supervision.

MEDICINE FOR DEPRESSION

Tricyclic antidepressants include some of the oldest ones we have. They block the absorption (reuptake) of the neurotransmitters, serotonin and norepinephrine, increasing the levels to these neurotransmitters in the brain. Tricyclic antidepressants also affect other chemical messengers, which can lead to a number of side effects. The generic versions of these medications are Amitriptyline, Amoxapine, Desipramine, Doxepin, Imipramine,

Nortryptline, Protriptyline, and Triamipraine. Trazadone is called an antidepressant and might be considered a sleep aid (and is non-addictive).

Monoamine Oxidase Inhibitors (also called MAOIs) block the actions of monoamine oxidase enzymes. MAOIs are responsible for breaking down neurotransmitters such as dopamine, norepinephrine, and serotonin in the brain. MAOIs are typically only used when other antidepressants have proven ineffective, because they have a higher risk of drug interactions than standard antidepressants and can also interact with certain types of food such as aged cheeses and cured meats. They also tend to have more side effects than standard antidepressants, and may cause a withdrawal syndrome upon discontinuation.

Selegiline (EMSAM) is administered by way of a patch. The EMSAM patch is a unique MAOI, being the only antidepressant utilizing a transdermal delivery system. This was welcomed by clinicians who hoped that EMSAM would be better tolerated than oral MAOIs and non-MAOI antidepressants, as well as being effective for treatment in a wide spectrum of depressed patients including atypical depression, bipolar depression, and refractory depression. Unfortunately, the clinical use of EMSAM has been underutilized and its potential usefulness overlooked.

SUPPLEMENTS FOR THE
TREATMENT OF MENTAL ILLNESS

It is advised that anyone trying these supplements should ask their doctor about how they may interfere with other medications they are on. This includes psychotropic medications.

Fish oil contains omega-3 fatty acids called docosahexaenoic acid (DHA) and eicosapentaenoic acid (EPA). DHA and EPA are sometimes called the marine omega-3s because they mainly come from fish. Some of the best fish to eat to obtain fish oil from in your diet include wild-caught salmon, herring, white fish, sardines and anchovies. Some nuts, seeds, and vegetable oils contain alpha-linolenic acid (ALA), which may be converted to DHA and EPA in the body.

When you purchase an omega-3 fatty acid supplement, look on the back of the pill container to see the amount of DHA/EPA it contains. If it doesn't list it, I would not buy it. The higher the numbers, the more expensive the fish oil is. Your physician can write you a prescription for fish oil. You should talk to him or her about the efficacy and safety of omega-3s and DHA/EPA.

An international evidence review has found that certain nutritional supplements can increase the effectiveness of antidepressants for people with clinical depression. Omega 3 fish oils, S-adenosylmethionine (SAMe), methylfolate (bio active form of folate) and Vitamin D, were all found to boost the effects of medication.

University of Melbourne and Harvard researchers examined forty clinical trials worldwide, alongside a systematic review of the evidence for using nutrient supplements (known as nutraceuticals) to treat clinical depression in tandem with antidepressants such as SSRIs, SNRIs and tricyclic medication.

Head of the ARCADIA Mental Health Research Group at the University of Melbourne, Dr. Jerome Sarris, led the meta-analysis, and published it in the American Journal of Psychiatry. Dr. Sarris said "The strongest finding from our review was that Omega 3 fish oil in combination with antidepressants had a statistically significant effect over a placebo. . . . Many studies have shown Omega 3s are very good for general brain health and improving mood, but this is the first analysis of studies that looks at using them in combination with antidepressant medication. The difference for patients taking both antidepressants and Omega 3, compared to a placebo, was highly significant. This is an exciting finding because here we have a safe, evidence-based approach that could be considered a mainstream treatment."[106]

The University of Melbourne research team also found good evidence for methylfolate, Vitamin D, and SAMe as mood-enhancing therapy when taken with antidepressants. They reported mixed results for zinc, vitamin C, and tryptophan (an amino acid). Folic acid didn't work particularly well, nor did inositol.

Dr. Sarris said "A large proportion of people who have depression do not reach remission after one or two courses of antidepressant medication, Millions of people in Australia and hundreds of millions worldwide currently take antidepressants. There's real potential here to improve the mental health of people who have an inadequate response to them."[107]

Antioxidants are a class of chemicals that destroy free radicals in the bloodstream. There has been some critical research in the last twenty years that antioxidants help heal damaged mitochondria in the brain cells, as well as protect cells against cardiovascular disease and certain cancers. It also may help problems with mind and mood. Foods containing antioxidants include fruits such as blueberries, strawberries, raspberries, bananas, apples, and plums; and vegetables such as tomatoes, carrots, and broccoli, Eating the recommended 1 1/2 to 2 cups of fruits and two to three cups of vegetables per day can help ensure that various antioxidants are consumed and utilized by the body. Add berries to oatmeal or cereal at breakfast, sliced tomatoes on a sandwich at lunch, a fresh plum as a snack and toss some carrots and broccoli into a stir-fry at dinner to achieve an antioxidant-rich day.

There is some debate over whether you can get you required amount of antioxidants in medication. Under advice of my psychiatrist, I have taken multi-vitamins for years. I believe that they have helped me to not have some residual depression symptoms. There are some great scientific books on the subject.

The supplement 5-HTP (5-Hydroxytryptophan) is a chemical byproduct of the protein building block L-tryptophan, and increases the brain chemical serotonin. It is used for sleep disorders such as insomnia, depression, anxiety, migraine and tension-type headaches, fibromyalgia, obesity, premenstrual syndrome (PMS), premenstrual dysphoric disorder (PMDD), attention deficit-hyperactivity disorder (ADHD), seizure disorder, and Parkinson's disease.

ANTIPSYCHOTIC MEDICATIONS

Antipsychotic medications are just what the name implies; they help fight against psychosis.

ANTIPSYCHOTIC MEDICATIONS		
Brand Name	**Generic**	**Class**
Abilify	Aripiprazole	Atypical
Clozaril	Clozapine	Atypical
Fanapt	Iloperidone	Atypical
Geodon	Ziprasidone	Atypical
Haldol	Haloperidol	Conventional
Invega	Paliperidone	Atypical
Latuda	Lurasidone	Atypical
Mellaril	Thioridazine	Conventional
Moban	Molindone	Conventional
Navane	Thiothixene	Conventional
Prolixin	Fluphenazine	Conventional
Risperdal	Risperidone	Atypical
Rexulti	Brexpiprazole	Atypical
Saphris	Asenapine	Atypical
Seroquel	Quetiapine	Atypical
Stelazine	Trifluiperazine	Conventional
Thorazine	Chlorpromazine	Conventional
Zyprexa	Olanzapine	Atypical

Antipsychotic drugs have two major classifications; conventional or atypical. The atypical are the newer antipsychotics. Conventional or atypical antipsychotics work to treat symptoms of schizophrenia and the manic phase of bipolar disorder. Several atypical antipsychotics have a broader spectrum of action than conventional medications and are used for treating bipolar depression or depression that has not responded to treatment. The old anti-psychotics present a potentially dangerous side effect to the patient called tardive dyskinesia, which causes stiff, jerky, uncontrollable movements of the face and body.

Injectable antipsychotics are called long-acting antipsychotics or LAIs. They are important in helping patients who have a lack of insight about their illness (anosognosia). Injectables last longer than pills and help immensely when a person is not inclined to take medications orally.

MOOD STABILIZERS, AND ANTICONVULSANTS USED AS MOOD STABILIZERS

Lithium was discovered to be useful in treating bipolar disorder by an Australian, John Cade, in 1949. It has been in use in modern medicine for almost seventy years and as such has been tried and tested across the full range of mood disorders. Lithium, as a drug, is in a class by itself and many say it is the only true mood stabilizer. Other medications may be termed as such but lithium is the only drug, technically, of that class. Lithium is FDA-approved for use in bipolar mania and bipolar maintenance treatment often in combination with other medications. Lithium has substantial antisuicidal properties.

MOOD STABILIZERS, AND ANTICONVULSANTS USED AS MOOD STABILIZERS

Brand Name	Generic Name	Used As	Class	Suggested Adult Daily Dosage Range
Eskalith CR 450 Lithobid Lithonate Lithotab	Lithium Carbonate	Mood stabilizer for bipolar disorder	The earliest and most effective mood stabilizer for mania and preventing future bipolar episodes	Effective range blood levels monitored to maintain 0.8-1.2 mEQ/L
Depakote Depakote ER	Valproic Acid	Used to treat bipo-lar disorder	Anticonvulsive	See physician
Lamictal (lamotrigine)	Lamotrigine	Used to treat bipo-lar disorder	Anticonvulsive	See physician

MOOD STABILIZERS, AND ANTICONVULSANTS USED AS MOOD STABILIZERS

Brand Name	Generic Name	Used As	Class	Suggested Adult Daily Dosage Range
Neurontin	Gabapentin	Used to treat bipolar disorder	Anticonvulsive	See physician
Trileptal	Oxcarbazepine	Used to treat bipolar disorder	Anticonvulsive	See physician
Tegretol	Carbamazepine	Used to treat bipolar disorder	Anticonvulsive	See physician
Topamax	Topiramate	Used to treat bipolar disorder	Anticonvulsive	See physician

Over the years of lithium's success, those for whom it was prescribed showed great improvement. Many had been living in state hospitals for years and the discovery of a few new antidepressants along with lithium enabled these patients to be released into society. Lithium has specificity for mood disorders, with proven efficacy in the treatment of both unipolar depression and bipolar disorder.

ANTICONVULSANTS

One of the main groups of medications that are used as mood stabilizers were anticonvulsant medications. They were originally developed to treat seizures, but they were found to help control unstable moods as well. Two anticonvulsants commonly used as a mood stabilizer are valproic acid and Depakote (divalproex sodium). For some people, especially those with "mixed" symptoms of mania and depression or those with rapid-cycling bipolar disorder, valproic acid may work better than lithium.

ATYPICAL ANTIPSYCHOTICS USED AS MOOD STABILIZERS

Mood stabilizers are medications that moderate the manic highs and the depressed lows of bipolar disorder. Mood stabilizers are used primarily to treat the mood swings and depression of bipolar disorder.

ATYPICAL ANTIPSYCHOTICS USED AS MOOD STABILIZERS

Brand name	Generic Name	Used As	Class	Suggested Dose
Abilify (injectable also available)	Aripiprazole	Mood stabilizer	Atypical antipsychotic	See physician
Geodon	Ziprasidone	Mood stabilizer	Atypical antipsychotic	See physician
Latuda	Lurasidone	Mood stabilizer	Atypical antipsychotic	See physician
Risperdal (injectable also available)	Risperidone	Mood stabilizer	Atypical antipsychotic	See physician
Seroquel	Quetiapine	Mood stabilizer	Atypical antipsychotic	See physician
Zyprexa (injectable also available)	Olanzapine	Mood stabilizer	Atypical antipsychotic	See physician

ADHD MEDICATIONS

Drug Name	Generic	Duration
Adderall	Dextroamphetamine Sulf-Saccharate	4–6 hours
Adderall XR	Dextroamphetamine Sulf-Saccharate	8–12 hours
Aptensio XR	Methylphenidate HCL	10–12 hours
Concerta	Methylphenidate	8–12 hours
Daytrana transdermal patch	Methylphenidate	Up to 10 hours
Dexedrine	Dextroamphetamine Sulfate	4–6 hours
Dexedrine Spansule	Dextroamphetamine Sulfate	6–8 hours
Eveko	Amphetamine Sulfate	6 hours
Focalin	Dexmethylphenidate HCL	4–6 hours
Focalin XR	Dexmethylophenidate HCL	6–10 hours
Metadate CD	Methylphenidate HCL	6–8 hours
Medadate ER	Methylphenidate HCL	6–8 hours
Methylin	Methylphenidate HCL	3–4 hours

ADHD MEDICATIONS

Drug Name	Generic	Duration
Methylin ER	Methylphenidate HCL	6–8 hours
Ritalin	Methylphenidate HCL	3–4 hours
Ritalin LA	Methylphenidate HCL	8–10 hours
Ritalin SR	Methylphenidate HCL	4–8 hours
Quillivant	Methylphenidate HCL	12 hours
Vyvanse	Lisdexamfetamine Dimesylate	10–12 hours

ADHD MEDICATIONS—NON-STIMULANTS

Drug Name	Generic	Duration
Catapres	Clonidine HCL	4-6 hours
Catapres –TTS patch	Clonidine	Up to 7 days
Intuniv	Guanfacine HCL	24 hours
Kapvay	Clonidine HCL	12 hours
Strattera	Atomoxetine HCL	24 hours
Tenex	Guanfacine HCL	6-8 hours

COMMON BENZODIAZEPINES AND OTHER ANTI-ANXIETY DRUGS

Brand name	Generic name	Used as	Class	Suggested Dosage
Ativan	Lorazepam	Anti-anxiety	Benzodiazepine	See physician
Buspar	Buspirone	Anti-anxiety (Non-addictive)	Independent	See physician
Inderal	Propranolol	Anti-anxiety	Beta Blocker	See physician
Klonopin	Clonazepam	Anti-anxiety	Benzodiazepine	See physician
Xanax & XR	Alprazolam	Anti-anxiety	Benzodiazepine	See physician

Most prescriptions for benzodiazepines are written by nonpsychiatrists. The most common uses of benzodiazepines are to treat anxiety and sleep problems. While effective for both conditions, the medications have risks, especially when used over long periods. Long-term use can lead to dependence and withdrawal symptoms. In the elderly, research has shown that benzodiazepines can impair cognition, mobility, driving skills, and they increase the risk of falls.

APPENDIX C:
HOLMES-RAHE STRESS SCALE

Adults

To measure stress according to the Holmes-Rahe Stress Scale, the numbers of "life change units" that apply to events in the past year of an individual's life are added, and the final score gives a rough estimate of how stress affects health.

Life Event	Life Change Units
Vacation	13
Trouble with in-laws	29
Trouble with boss	23
Spouse starts or stops work	26
Sexual difficulties	39
Revision of personal habits	24
Retirement	45
Pregnancy	40
Personal injury or illness	53
Outstanding personal achievement	28
Minor violation of law	11
Minor mortgage or loan	17
Marriage	50
Marital separation	65
Marital reconciliation	45
Major mortgage	32
Major holiday	12
Imprisonment	63

Life Event	Life Change Units
Gain a new family member	39
Foreclosure of mortgage or loan	30
Divorce	73
Dismissal from work	47
Death of a spouse	100
Death of a close friend	37
Death of a close family member	63
Child leaving home	29
Change to different line of work	36
Change in working hours or conditions	20
Change in social activities	18
Change in sleeping habits	16
Change in schools	20
Change in responsibilities at work	29
Change in residence	20
Change in recreation	19
Change in number of family reunions	15
Change in living conditions	25
Change in health of family member	44
Change in frequency of arguments	35
Change in financial state	38
Change in eating habits	15
Change in church activities	19
Business readjustment	39
Beginning or end school	26

Score of 300+:   At risk of illness
Score of 150–299: Risk of illness is moderate (reduced by 30% from the above risk)
Score <150:   Only has a slight risk of illness

Non-adults

A modified scale has also been developed for non-adults. Similar to the adult scale, stress points for life events in the past year are added and compared to the rough estimate of how stress affects health.

Life Event	Life Change Units
Death of parent	100
Unplanned pregnancy/abortion	100
Getting married	95
Divorce of parents	90
Acquiring a visible deformity	80
Fathering a child	70
Jail sentence of parent for over one year	70
Marital separation of parents	69
Death of a brother or sister	68
Change in acceptance by peers	67
Unplanned pregnancy of sister	64
Discovery of being an adopted child	63
Marriage of parent to stepparent	63
Death of a close friend	63
Having a visible congenital deformity	62
Serious illness requiring hospitalization	58
Failure of a grade in school	56
Not making an extracurricular activity	55
Hospitalization of a parent	55
Jail sentence of parent for more than 30 days	53
Breaking up with boyfriend or girlfriend	53
Beginning to date	51
Suspension from school	50
Becoming involved with drugs or alcohol	50
Birth of a brother or sister	50

Life Event	Life Change Units
Increase in arguments between parents	47
Loss of job by parent	46
Outstanding personal achievement	46
Change in parent's financial status	45
Accepted at college of choice	43
Being a senior in high school	42
Hospitalization of a sibling	41
Increased absence of parent from home	38
Brother or sister leaving home	37
Addition of third adult to family	34
Becoming a full-fledged member of a church	31
Decrease in arguments between parents	27
Decrease in arguments with parents	26
Mother or father beginning work	26

Score of 300+:   At risk of illness
Score of 150–299: Risk of illness is moderate (reduced by 30% from the above risk)
Score <150:   Slight risk of illness

BIBLIOGRAPHY

American Psychiatric Association: *Diagnostic and Statisticians Manual of Mental Disorders,* 5th ed., text revision. Washington, DC: American Psychiatric Press, 2013.

Brooks, Thomas. *Precious Remedies against Satan's Devices.* Vol. 1 of *The Works of Thomas Brooks.* London: James Nisbet, 1861. See also related sermons in this two-volume collection of Brooks' writings.

Charney, Dennis S., Pamela Skylar, Joseph Buxam, and Eric Nestler, eds. *Neurobiology of Mental Illness,* 4th ed. Oxford: Oxford University Press, 2013.

Edwards, Jonathan. *A Treatise of Religious Affections* (1746). *The Works of Jonathan Edwards, Vol. 2: Religious Affections.* Edinburgh: Banner of Truth Trust, 1974. See also The Ethereal Library https://www.ccel.org/ccel/edwards/affections.html.

Goodwin, Thomas. "A Child of Light Walking in Darkness" *The Works of Thomas Goodwin,* 5 vols. London: James Nisbet, 1861, 3.235–350.

Jefferson, Charles. *The Minister as Shepherd.* Hong Kong: Living Books for All, 1984.

Keller, Phillip. *A Shepherd's Looks at Psalm 23.* Grand Rapids: Zondervan, 1970.

Lloyd-Jones, D. Martyn. *Commentaries on Ephesians 5; The Christian Warfare; Commentaries on Ephesians 6; The Christian Soldier.* Grand Rapids: Baker Book House, 1976.

Lloyd-Jones, D. Martyn. *Healing and the Scriptures.* Nashville: Thomas Nelson. 1982.

Lombardo, Gregory. *Understanding the Mind of Your Bipolar Child*: New York: St. Martin's Press, 2006.

Newman, Barbara M. and Phillip R. *Development through Life, a Psychosocial Approach.* Homewood, IL: Dorsey Press, 1984.

Pink, A. W. *Exposition of the Gospel of John,* Volume 3. Grand Rapids: Zondervan, 1975.

Robertson, A. T. *Robertson Word Studies, of the New Testament,* www. biblestudytools.com/commentaries/robertsons-word-pictures.

Sibbes, Richard. *The Bruised Reed and the Smoking Flax* (1630). Volume 1 of *The Complete Works of Richard Sibbes.* Edinburgh: Banner of Truth, 1973.

Torrey, E. Fuller. *Freudian Fraud: The Malignant Effect of Freud's Theory on American Thought and Culture*: New York: Harper Collins, 1992.

WEBSITES

Johns Hopkins Hospital, http://www.hopkinsmedicine.org/psychiatry/ specialty_areas/eating_disorders/faq.htm, accessed May 2017.

Mayo Clinic, http://www.mayoclinic.org/diseases-conditions, accessed May 2017.

ENDNOTES

1. D. Martyn Lloyd-Jones, *Healing and the Scriptures* (Nashville: Thomas Nelson Publishers, 1982), 7

2. In the Greek it is, ωουδεν υπεστειλαμεn. It is in the middle voice and is translated, "to withdraw oneself, to cower, to shrink, to conceal, and to dissemble."

3. The Greek word αντεχομενον. It is in the present middle participle of αντεχω, old verb, "to hold back, in middle to hold oneself face to face with, to cling to," as in 1 Thessalonians 5:14.

4. The faithful word (του πιστου λογου). See Romans 16:17; 1 Timothy 1:15; 1 Timothy 6:3. Some would see a reference here to Christ as the Personal Logos.

5. The Greek word παρακαλειν. This means to come alongside and encourage. It has to be exhorting, using sound doctrine. This would be the building (trowel) aspect of the pastor; to call to one's side, call for, summon to address, speak to, (call to, call upon), which may be done in the way of exhortation, entreaty, comfort, instruction, etc.

6. εφλεϖγχειν. Gerhard Kittel. *Theological Dictionary of the New Testament* (TDNT), Volume 2 (Grand Rapids: Eerdmans, 1964, 474. It means "to show someone his sin and to summon to repentance."

7. του αντιλεγοντα. This is literally, to speak against; present active participle of αντιλεγω, old word, to answer back, as in Romans 10:21: "The talkers back." I believe that you should be aware that one of the best books I have read on human development; it is by a husband and wife team, Newman, Barbara M. and Phillip Newman *Development through Life, a Psychosocial Approach* (Homewood, IL: Dorsey Press, 1984).

8. καθ υπερβολην υπερ δυναμιν εβαρηθημεν Old verb from βαρο, weight, βαρυ, weighty. This is a first aorist passive indicative. It was beyond Paul's power to endure, if left to him. Paul is a transparent about his sufferings.

9. "Indeed, we had the sentence within ourselves;" The word "had" is the regular perfect of εχηϭ to have. The perfect tense is a past completed action with continuous results in the present. The Apostle and his missionary team still had the vivid recollection of that experience (Acts 2:13). That we should not trust in ourselves (ινα μη πεποιθοτε ωμεν επ εαυτοι) "This dreadful trial was sent to him in order to give him a precious spiritual lesson" (Acts 12:7–10; Robertson and Plummer, *A Critical and Exegetical Commentary on the First Epistle of St. Paul to the Corinthians* [New York: Scribner's, 1911]). Note periphrastic perfect active subjunctive of πειθω, to persuade. In (επι), upon both ourselves and God.

10. εκ τηλικουτου θανατου, "Out of so great a death." He had considered himself as good as dead. The word delivered is (ερυσατο) will deliver (ρυσεται). Old verb ρυω, middle, ρυομαι, draw oneself, as out of a pit, rescue. So Paul faces death without fear. On whom we have set our hope (ειον ηλπικαμεν). Perfect active indicative of ελπιζω. We still have that hope, emphasized by ετι ρυσεται. (He will still deliver.)

11. John Lange, *Commentary on the Holy Scriptures* (2 Cor. 1:8–11). http://classicchristianlibrary. com/library/lange_johann/Langes_v26-Lange-Rev.pdf (accessed 2/10/18).

12. *Christianity Today,* http://www.christianitytoday.com/history/issues/issue-89/english-puritans-christian-history-timeline.html (accessed 2/10/18).

13. Joel Beeke, "Reading the Puritans," *Union Theology*. https://www.uniontheology.org/resources/historical/reading-the-puritans (accessed 2/12/18).

14. *Anah*, to be put down, become low, to be depressed, to be downcast, to be afflicted, to stoop.

15. Donald Henry and Maurice Spence-Jones, *Pulpit Commentary* (New York, Trubner & Company, 1897).

16. Charles Spurgeon, *Consolation for the Despairing*, Public domain.

17. βοσκε τα αρνια μου. For the old word βοσκω (to feed as a herdsman) see Matthew 8:33. Present active imperative here. Αρνια is a diminutive of αρνο (lamb).

18. Feed my sheep (βοσκε τα προβατια). Many manuscripts read προβατα (sheep) instead of προβατια (little sheep or lambs).

19. A.W. Pink, *Exposition of the Gospel of John*, Volume 3 (Grand Rapids: Zondervan, 1975), 319. That he may be "converted" by it, turned from that dangerous self-confidence to consciousness of his inability to trust himself, even for a moment. Here Satan is foiled and made to serve the purpose of that grace which he hates and resists. He can overpower the self-sufficient Peter; but only to fling him for relief on His omnipotent Lord. Just as the "messenger of Satan" to buffet Paul (2 Cor. 12:7) only works for what he in nowise desires, to repress the pride, so ready to spring up in us, and which the lifting up to the third heavens might tend to foster. Here there had been no fall and all was over-ruled for fullest blessing; in Peter's case, on the other hand, Satan's effort would be to assail the fallen disciple with suggestions of a sin too great to be forgiven, or at least, for restoration to that eminent place from which it would be torture to remember he had fallen. What he needed to meet this with was faith; and this, therefore, the Lord prays, might not fail him.

20. Steve Bloem and Robyn. *Broken Minds, Hope for Healing When You Feel Like You're Losing It* (Grand Rapids: Kregel, 2005), 155–156.

21. Charles Jefferson, *The Minister as Shepherd* (Hong Kong: Living Books for All, 1984), 129–130.

22. The encouragement of the fainthearted, in this text, as it is in most of the New Testament texts with (παρα μυτηεομαι) indicates that comfort for the fainthearted is God's comfort through the Christian community (Kittel, TDNT, 816–823). It cannot be emphasized enough that support groups for the mentally ill, done in the right fashion, will help accomplish the strengthening and edification of the mentally ill and their families. As a shepherd, God's man can give great comfort and teach others who do so. Why is it tempting, at times, to warn the fainthearted and encourage the unruly?

23. The writer is saying that the human spirit given by God is resilient and helps people get through all kinds of sicknesses. But when the spirit, itself, is wounded or broken, there is much to endure and no inner resource to help endure it. Spirit is used here for the person's inner being. If your spirit is broken, then you cannot endure; you cannot sustain the sickness. Proverbs doesn't offer a solution for this dilemma nor does the writer go into reasons why the spirit may be wounded. It simply makes a statement: When the healing mechanism is what needs to be healed, that's a serious problem. A broken spirit whatever the cause, puts a person into the category of not being able to go with life in a normal fashion.

24. Charles Edward Jefferson, *The Minister as Shepherd*, 43–44.

25. William Carey Quotes. BrainyQuote.com, Xplore Inc, 2018. https://www.brainyquote.com/quotes/william_carey_191985, accessed March 19, 2018.

26. The Hebrew word for terror is *eymah*. The NASB uses the following English words for *eymah*: dread, fear, fearsome, terrible, terror and terrors.

27. Hebrew transliteration (*hashekah)*, in a prose section is in Genesis 15:12. There is a "supernatural darkness" paralleled by the Hebrew word *tardema*, meaning "deep sleep" or "torpor." Psalm 83:5 and 139:12 contain *hashekah*; in fact, 139:12 also has *hoshek*. Both refer to a darkness that cannot hide or limit God. The word appears twice in Isaiah. In 8:22 it is parallel to *sara* (distress), *mupsuqa* (anguished gloom), and *apela m nuddah* (thick blackness).

28. *Tsalmaveth*: Death-shadow, deep shadow, deep darkness, shadow of death, death-shadow, death-shadow, deep shadow, darkness, death-shadow (of distress, extreme danger), death-shadow (of place of the dead). It is used eighteen times in the NASB, translated "black gloom," one time; "dark," one time; "deep darkness," six times; "deep shadow," four times; "shadow of death," four times; "thick darkness," two times.

29. Heartfelt Counseling Ministries has many programs that will equip you to help those who have mental illness and those who care for someone with mental illness. This book is part of our commitment to help. We have seminars and written material for you to successfully help missionaries, pastoral staff and congregants to deal with depression, panic disorder, bipolar, schizophrenia, and other disturbances of the mind and mood.

30. Charles Spurgeon, "The Child of Light Walking in Darkness," *Christian Classics Ethereal Library*,Public domain, https://www.ccel.org/ccel/spurgeon/sermons33.xlviii.html?highlight =child,of,god,walking,in,darkness#highlight (accessed 2/12/18).

31. In his exposition of Psalm 40, Spurgeon says, "When our Lord bore in His own person the terrible curse which was due sin, He was so cast down as to be like prisoner in a deep, dark, fearful dungeon, amid whose horrible glooms the captive heard a noise as onrushing torrents, while overhead resounded the tramp of furious foes. Our Lord in His anguish was like a captive in the oubliettes, dungeon with an opening only at the top) forgotten of all mankind, immured amid horror, darkness, and desolation. Yea the Lord Jehovah made Him to ascend from all His abasement. He retraced His steps from that deep hell of anguish into which He had been cast as our substitute. He, who thus delivered our surety in extremis, will not fail to liberate us from our lighter griefs." Spurgeon, Charles, *Treasury of David*, vol .1 (1869 repr, Newark, N.J. Cornerstone, n.d.) 261–62.

32. John Owen, *Christolgia*, 1679. Public domain.

33. That no advantage may be gained over us (ινα μη πλεονεκτηθωμεν). First aorist passive subjunctive after ινα μη (negative purpose) of πλεονεκτεω, old verb from πλεονεκτη, a covetous man (2 Corinthians 5:10), to take advantage of, to gain, to overreach. In NT, only in 2 Corinthians 2:11; 7:2; 12:17; 1 Thessalonians 4:6. "That we may not be overreached by Satan." His devices (αυτου τα νοηματα). Νοημα from νοεω to use the νου is old word, especially for evil plans and purposes as here.

34. So that on the contrary (ωστε τουναντιον). The natural result expressed by ωστε and the infinitive. Τουναντιον is by crasis for το εναντιον and accusative of general reference. Rather (μαλλον). Absent in some MSS. lest by any means (μη πω). Negative purpose. Swallowed up (καταποθη). First aorist passive subjunctive of καταπινω, to drink down (1 Corinthians 15:54). With his overmuch sorrow (τηε περισσοτεραι λυπη). Instrumental case, "by the more abundant sorrow" (comparative of adjective(περισσο).

35. The Greek word for sober Νηπϖψατε, means "to be sober, to be calm and collected in spirit to be temperate, dispassionate, and circumspect." The word "alert" is γρηγορησατε. It is a first aorist active imperative of γρηγορεω, late present imperative from perfect εγρηγορα (to be awake) from εγειρω (to arouse), as in Matthew 24:42.

36. καταπινο

37. Lloyd Jones, *The Christian Warfare* (Grand Rapids, Baker Book House, 1977).

38. The Society for Development and Behavioral Pediatrics has a list of clinicians. http://www.sdbp.org/about-us (accessed 2/10/18),

39. Child Neurology Society, http://www.childneurologysociety.org/

40. Charles Spurgeon, one of the most quoted pastors in the world, wrote a classic book called The Saint and the Savior (Pasadena, TX: Pilgrim Books, 1975). Two important chapters are chapter 10, "Jesus Hiding Himself," and chapter 11, "The Causes for Apparent Desertion." The following causes are listed:

    • Divine Sovereignty manifested is communion of the saints with our Lord.

    • Without this the believer could not enter into the depths of fellowship with Christ in His sufferings.

- Thus, in some men the Lord works a preparation for eminent service.
- The Lord Jesus sometimes hides Himself from us, because by this foresight and prudence he is thus able to prevent the breaking forth of evil.
- Our Lord Jesus designs us also to try our faith.
- A temporary withdrawal endears Christ to us upon His return, and gives the soul some idea of the infinite value of His smile.
- This also whets our appetite for heaven and makes us thirst for the land of bliss.
- Gross and foul offenses of any kind will drive the King from the soul very speedily.
- Careless living, even if we fall not into open transgression, will soon build a wall between our Lord and the soul.
- Idleness in the ways of grace will also hinder communion.
- Unthankfulness will soon strip us from our joys.
- Cowardice will also rob us of the Master's manifest presence.
- Harshness to the afflicted may bring us into deep waters.
- Pride cast thick shadow over any believer who indulges in it.
- Idolatrous love whatever may be the object of it, is so abominable, that it will shut out the light of God's countenance in a short space, unless it be destroyed.
- Unbelief, distrust, and worldly care will also provoke him to return unto His place.
- But carnal security is the master-sin in this point.

41. Charles Spurgeon, one of the most quoted pastors in the world, wrote a classic book called, *The Saint and the Savior*. It was published by Pilgrim Books, Pasadena Texas

42. Philip W. Gold, "Can Depression Be Cured? New Research on Depression and Its Treatments," Library of Congress Symposium, May 5, 2016, http://stream-media.loc.gov/webcasts/captions/2016/160505klu1400.txt (accessed 2/10/18).

43. National Institute of Mental Health, "Schizophrenia," https://www.nimh.nih.gov/health/topics/schizophrenia/index.shtml#part_145426 (accessed 3/26/18).

44. Jordyn Taylor. "A Genetic Breakthrough Could Help Cure One of Our Most Misunderstood Ilnesses," *mic.com*, January 28, 2016, https://mic.com/articles/133742/a-genetic-breakthrough-could (accessed 2/10/18).

45. *2016 Children's Mental Health Report*, Child Mind Institute, https://childmind.org/report/2016-childrens-mentalhealth-report/mental-health-disorders-common/ (accessed 2/10/18).

46. Ibid.

47. "Research Domain Criteria (RDoC)," National Institute of Mental Health, https://www.nimh.nih.gov/research-priorities/rdoc/index.shtml (accessed 2/10/18).

48. Dennis Charney, Pamela Sklar, Joseph Buxbaum, and Eric Nestler, eds., *Neurobiology of Mental Illness*, 4th ed. (Oxford: Oxford Universoty Press, 2014), 520.

49. "Transcranial Magnetic Stimulation," Mayo Clinic, http://www.mayoclinic.org/tests-procedures/transcranial-magnetic-stimulation/home/ovc-20163795 (accessed 2/10/18).

50. *Neurobiology of Mental Illness*, 520.

51. "Deep Brain Stimulation," Parkinson's Foundation, http://www.parkinson.org/understanding-parkinsons/treatment/surgery-treatment-options/Deep-Brain-Stimulation (accessed 2/10/18).

52. *Neurobiology of Mental Illness*, 520.

53. Aan Het Rot M,. et al., "Ketamine for depression: where do we go from here?" *Biol. Psychiatry*. 2012 Oct 1;72(7):537–47.

54. Diaz Granados N., et al. "Rapid resolution of suicidal ideation after a single infusion of an N-methyl-D-aspartate antagonist in patients with treatment-resistant major depressive disorder." *J. Clin. Psychiatry*. 2010 Dec. 71(12):1605–11.

55. Rodriguez C. I., et al. "Randomized controlled crossover trial of ketamine in obsessive-compulsive disorder: proof-of-concept." *Neuropsychopharmacology.* 2013 Nov. 38(12):2475–83; Feder A., et al. "Efficacy of intravenous ketamine for treatment of chronic posttraumatic stress disorder: a randomized clinical trial." *JAMA Psychiatry.* 2014 Jun. 71(6):681–8.

56. Donald Klein and Paul Wender, *Mind, Mood and Medicine* (New York: New American Library, 1982), 250

57. "ADHD," Health Central, https://www.healthcentral.com/adhd (accessed 2/10/18).

58. Ibid.

59. American Psychiatric Association, *Diagnostic and Statistical Manual of Mental Disorders* (DSM–5) (Washington DC: American Psychiatric Association, 2013), 11, 32, 59–66.

60. "Adult Attention-Deficit Disorder (ADHD)," Mayo Clinic, https://www.mayoclinic.org/diseases-conditions/adult-adhd/symptoms-causes/syc-20350878

61. "The pattern of onset description might include information about early developmental delays or any losses of social or language skills. In cases where skills have been lost, parents or caregivers may give a history of gradual or relatively rapid deterioration in social behaviors or language skills. Typically this would occur between 12 and 24 months of age and is distinguished from the rare instances of developmental regression occurring after at least 2 years of normal development (previously described as childhood disintegrative disorder)." American Psychiatric Association: *Diagnostic and Statisticians Manual of Mental Disorders*, 5th ed., text revision. Washington, DC: American Psychiatric Press, 2013, DSM–5, 55.

62. Ibid., 56–57.

63. "Autism Spectrum Disorder" National Institute of Mental Health, https://www.nimh.nih.gov/health/topics/autism-spectrum-disorders-asd/index.shtml#part_145438 (accessed 2/12/18

64. Newman & Newman, *Development through Life: A Psychosocial Approach* (Homewood: IL: The Dorsey Press, 1984). This is a good book, but the authors are unsaved. You should not accept every concept as being right, but should always "test all things," using the Bible as your foundation and guide.

65. Marsha Linehan, *Skills Training Manual for Treating Borderline Personality Disorder.* (New York/London: Guilford Press, 1993).

66. "Bulimia Nervosa: Causes, Symptoms, Signs and Treatment Help" Eating Disorder Hope, https://www.eatingdisorderhope.com/information/bulimia#What-is-bulimia (accessed 2/13/18

67. "The lasting impact of neglect," American Psychological Association, http://www.apa.org/monitor/2014/06/neglect.aspx (accessed 2/13/18.

68. Those are just some of the problems that David A. Wolfe, PhD, a psychologist at the University of Toronto, and his former student Kathryn L. Hildyard, PhD, detailed in a 2002 review (*Child Abuse & Neglect*, 2002).

69. DSM–5, 169–170.

70. Ibid., 170.

71. Ibid., 223.

72. Jefferson, *The Minister as Shepherd*, 48–49.

73. This was said to Steve by the Chair of Psychiatry at the University of Kansas, Dr. Donald Goodwin

74. For more information on medications for depression, please see our chart on page 147 of this book. You can also go online to the FDA or NIMH website, as well as Medline, Mayo Clinic. There is good information in nursing books for purchase or borrowed from your local library.

75. *Neurobiology of Mental Illness,* 225–228

76. Ibid., 646.

77. Ibid.

78. Ibid., 532.

79. Some of the above has been used from https://www.med.unc.edu/psych/wmd/mood-disorders/perinatal#md_pregnancy (accessed 2/10/18).

80. "Postpartum Depression and Suicide," *suicide.org*, http://www.suicide.org/postpartum-depression-and-suicide.html (accessed 2/13/18).

81. "Perinatal Psychiatry Inpatient Unit," UNC School of Medicine, https://www.med.unc.edu/psych/wmd/patient_care/perinatal-inpatient (accessed 2/13/18).

82. This was quoted on the following website: *FactsForHealth.org*, The Anxiety and Depression Association of America http://www.factsforhealth.org/ptsd.html

83. "Posttraumatic Stress Disorder," National Alliance of Mental Illness, https://www.nami.org/Learn-More/Mental-Health-Conditions/Posttraumatic-Stress-Disorder#sthash.7ku5evwB.dpuf (accessed 2/13/18).

84. Ibid.

85. DSM–5, 271.

86. "Posttraumatic Stress Disorder," *NHS Choices*, http://www.nhs.uk/Conditions/Post-traumatic-stress-disorder/Pages/Causes.aspx (accessed 2/13/18).

87. DSM–5, 173.

88. "Treating Premenstrual Dysphoric Disorder," *Harvard Mental Health Letter*, October 2009, http://www.health.harvard.edu/womens-health/treating-premenstrual-dysphoric-disorder (accessed 2/10/18).

89. "Schizoaffective Disorder," National Alliance of Mental Illness, https://www.nami.org/Learn-More/Mental-Health-Conditions/Schizoaffective (accessed 2/13/18).

90. Traci Pederson, "Flat Affect," *PsychCentral*, https://psychcentral.com/encyclopedia/flat-affect/ (accessed 2/13/18).

91. *Neurobiology of Mental Illness*, 225–228.

92. "Schizophrenia" National Alliance of Mental Illness, https://www.nimh.nih.gov/health/publications/schizophrenia-basics/tr-15-3517_155669.pdf (accessed 2/13/18).

93. *SADA*, http://www.sada.org.uk/index_2.php/ (accessed 2/13/18).

94. Elinore F. McCance-Katz, M.D., Ph.D., https://blog.samhsa.gov/tag/mental-health-2/#.WrErjsPwa70 (accessed 3/26/18).

95. Sabrina Tavernise, "U.S. Suicide Rate Surges to a 30-Year High," *The New York Times*, https://www.nytimes.com/2016/04/22/health/us-suicide-rate-surges-to-a-30-year-high.html?_r=0 (accessed 2/10/18).

96. Steve Bloem and Robyn Bloem, *CAMI Leaders Guide* (Grand Rapids, MI: Heartfelt Counseling Ministries, 2007).

97. World Health Organization, 2018, "Suicide," http://www.who.int/mediacentre/factsheets/fs398/en/ (accessed 3/26/18).

98. "Fast Facts," Treatment Advocacy Center, http://www.treatmentadvocacycenter.org/evidence-and-research/fast-facts (accessed 2/13/18).

99. Ronald Fieve, *Mood Swing: The Third Revolution in Psychiatry* (New York: Bantam, 1979).

100. Peter D. Kramer, *Listening to Prozac* (New York: Penguin, 1993).

101. John MacArthur, *Our Sufficiency in Christ: Three Deadly Influences That Undermine Your Spiritual Life* (Nashville: Word, 1991) 98–99.

102. Bosthwick, "Be Still My Soul" first published in *Hymns from the Land of Luther*, 1855.

103. Alva McCain, *The Greatness of the Kingdom* (Winona Lake, IN: BMH Books, 1959), 496.

104. Ibid., 496.

105. Andrew Solomon, The Noonday Demon: An Atlas of Depression (New York: Simon & Schuster, 2001), 56–57.

106. Jerome Sarris, et al.,"Adjunctive Nutraceuticals for Depression: A Systematic Review and Meta-Analyses" American Journal of Psychiatry, June 1, 2016, 173(6):575–8.7

107. Ibid.